# GEOCACHING IN THE UK

by
Terry Marsh

2 POLICE SQUARE, MILNTHORPE, CUMBRIA, LA7 7PY
www.cicerone.co.uk

Printed in China on behalf of Latitude Press Ltd
A catalogue record for this book is available from the British Library.
All photographs are by the author unless otherwise stated.

*This book is dedicated to my son, Martin, who casually dangled 'Why don't you write a book about geocaching?' in front of me, which drove me to discover the pursuit for myself.*

## ACKNOWLEDGEMENTS

Geocaching is a developing pursuit, and to give a meaningful overview I have called on a number of people who have kindly given me assistance in the writing of this book.

John Stead, one of the first geocachers in the UK, very generously offered to read the manuscript of the first edition, although I doubt he knew what he was letting himself in for. Nevertheless, he did so unfailingly and offered sensible advice as well as picking up on my errors. I continue to be grateful for his contribution.

Dave Palmer (deceangi), one of the most experienced and respected reviewers, made me an offer I couldn't refuse – to read through the manuscript. He gave me very helpful advice and some historical information, which was both appreciated and taken on board.

Groundspeak, the founding organisation, have given permission to use screenshots from the www.geocaching.com website, along with consent to use trademark logos. Although the symbol is not repeated throughout this book, Travel bug® is a registered trademark of Groundspeak. They have also generously supplied pictures of geocaching merchandise pages. The Geological Society of America has kindly given consent to use their guidelines for the placement of EarthCaches™, along with the EarthCache™ name (for which, also, the trademark symbol is not repeated throughout this book) and logos. Garmin UK have generously given permission to use illustrations of their GPS devices (page 21); Groundspeak, Trimble, Memory Map and SatMap have given permission to use images on page 23. The Geocaching Association of Great Britain (GAGB) have given permission to use images and text from their website – www.gagb.org.uk.

Others, especially colleagues in North West Caching, have helped in small but no less important ways, especially Cass Flowers (*geocass*) and Bernie Hughes (agentmancuso) and colleagues in the GAGB. Jeanette Hindle (lfc4eva) agreed to the use of her geocoin design shown on page 20; Ian Grime (lizzardman) gave consent to use his designs on pages 96, 97 and 138; members of the north-west community supplied many of the other colourful pictures of geocoins scattered across the margins of this book; and my son, Martin, took the photograph of my grandson on page 106, and of me on page 51.

Especial thanks goes to my wife, Viv, who says geocaching is the best thing we've ever done, because now we go out walking together much more often, and visit places neither of us have ever seen before.

*Front cover:* Geocaching is a great activity for families

# CONTENTS

## DISCLAIMER

Every effort has been made to ensure that the instructions and techniques in this book cover the subject safely and in full detail. However, the author and publishers cannot accept any responsibility for any accident, injury, loss or damage sustained while following any of the techniques described.

An EarthCache is a special place you can
visit to learn about a particular aspect of
Earth science – Malham Cove (Yorkshire
Dales National Park) is a perfect example

# INTRODUCTION

*...geocaching really is a good tourist guide too. You don't miss too much if you just let yourself be led by geocaching through a country.*

Patrick Liss (Myst0gan)

Everyone dreams of finding treasure – a crock of gold at the end of a rainbow, a rare antique of singular value or an undiscovered Wordsworth manuscript. Such is, indeed, the stuff of dreams. Yet the laws of probability dictate that it's extremely unlikely to happen.

For those with less exalted ambition, treasure is all around, just waiting to be found. What is more, accurate and detailed clues have been left as to where to find it. It may not bring life-changing riches, for the value of this treasure lies in its discovery – not in its quantifiable worth.

Geocaching is essentially a modern form of treasure hunting, which has, of course, been around for centuries. In its simplest form, it involves being given a list of objects to find and bring back, and the first one back with everything wins. A more sophisticated version involves unravelling clues to the whereabouts of hidden 'treasure' and then heading off to find it. The same holds true of the next stage in the development of the pursuit – letterboxing – which started on Dartmoor in 1854 and followed much the same principle.

With today's technology, treasure hunting has developed yet again into the activity of geocaching – a cross between treasure hunting and orienteering. Started in the US in the year 2000, when the first 'geocache' was hidden and its location posted on the internet for others to find with a GPS, geocaching has now become a worldwide phenomenon. (Indeed, in April 2014 the term 'geocaching' was officially recognised as a Scrabble word!)

Anyone can join in – all you need is access to the website where geocache locations are listed. Caches can be found almost on your own doorstep, and certainly within a short distance of where you live.

Simply choose a geocache, take your GPS and go out and find the spot. Once you get to its location, the fun really starts, as the geocache is often cleverly hidden. And it is important that no-one else (that is, a non-geocacher, or 'muggle' – a term borrowed from the *Harry Potter* books) sees you find it. It may be in a town or other busy place, but caches are more often hidden in the countryside. (All the full-page pictures in this book are of places where someone has placed a geocache or of locations that are EarthCaches.)

When you find the geocache – it's likely to be in a small plastic box – have a look at what's inside. It could be just a logbook to record your find, or there may be other items too. You can take these as your treasure, as long as you replace any items you take with others of equal or greater value. Then hide the cache (without any muggles seeing) where and how you found it, and go home to record your find on the website.

That's it (fundamentally, at least); there is no other achievement. But unlike trainspotting, for example, which is largely a chance activity, successful geocaching hinges on your own ability to find the location of the cache. With geocaching, you are the search engine.

But be warned: it is addictive. Once you find your first few caches, so the urge to find more grows, and every trip out (even in your local town) or visit to the countryside suddenly offers the possibility of finding another cache.

## WHAT'S IN A CACHE?
Many traditional caches contain trinkets, of no real value, which can be swapped ('take something out, put something in' is a founding rule). Other caches provide a series of clues that lead around notable sites – they may be of historical significance or perhaps illustrate aspects of rural life.

Caches may contain some items that have been invented specifically for the activity as it has grown. Known as 'Travel bugs' and 'geocoins', these items have a 'mission' assigned by the owner – usually to travel around the world via caches, or more specifically, for example, to visit mountains or other caches in an alphabetical sequence.

Once a Travel bug or geocoin has been retrieved from a cache, its discovery is logged on the geocaching website, where its own page and stated mission can be discovered. It is then for the finder to comply with the mission statement and move the item on accordingly. What makes this simple endeavour all the more appealing is that, via the website, the progress of each item can be tracked and displayed on a map, enabling children in particular to experience a lesson in regional, national and global geography.

## OTHER BENEFITS OF GEOCACHING
In addition to being a fun activity, there is a growing realisation that geocaching has a number of bolt-on benefits. Firstly, it need not be a solitary pursuit – many geocachers go out with friends or in family groups, involving children, parents and grandparents in the enjoyment of our countryside in a pleasurable and healthy way. It is also a great way to spend retirement days.

In parts of the country local geocachers organise social events – maybe a visit to a pub, or a walk to coincide with solstices or significant historical events. Such 'cache events' are commonplace, and provide yet another opportunity to socialise and interact with like-minded people.

Geocaching is for all the family – young and old alike

Geocaching keeps you in touch with nature – and with your friends! (photo: Mark Fishwick)

In fact, geocaching gets us all out walking and adds a new dimension to a walk. Often, the search for geocaches, even close to your home, will take you to places you probably never knew existed – a small local park, maybe, or a corner of woodland rarely visited.

Educationalists in the US, and organisations such as the National Trust and various local authorities in the UK, are using geocaching as a way of putting a new slant on learning by giving children GPS devices and getting them to navigate to a given location, where the teacher then explains the significance of the spot – in historical, geological or local terms – before moving on to the next location. Not only do the children get the lesson they were going to be given anyway, but they also learn how to handle new technology and to navigate using satellite systems. Learning suddenly acquires an additional level of interest.

Geocaching can also be useful as a team-building exercise for those in company management.

Today, it's mind-boggling to think that there are tens of thousands of geocaches within the UK, and over two million worldwide. So popular is the pursuit becoming that the number of new caches worldwide is increasing by more than a thousand every week, and there are more than two million 'finds' every month. Judging by the comments left in logbooks and on the website, huge fun and enjoyment is derived from it.

And whether you're searching near your home or on a visit to the countryside, you'll never look at your environment in the same way again. Every walk in the park with the dog, every trip to the countryside, and perhaps every visit to the supermarket leads past a concealed geocache that most folk would simply never know was there. So get out and see what treasure you can find!

The Cantilever, a fine EarthCache on the summit of Glyder Fach in Snowdonia National Park

# 1

# THE BASICS

## WHAT IS GEOCACHING?

Put simply, geocaching is a cross between treasure hunting and orienteering, but without the rush. It is, after all, a leisure pursuit – an adjunct to recreational walking that adds a new dimension to a visit to the countryside or even to the supermarket.

Typically, a 'cache' takes the form of a plastic Tupperware-like box – one that can be locked against the weather. But there are a number of different types of cache and not all of them are as obvious as a large plastic box. A cache is concealed, often ingeniously, in some not-easy-to-stumble-upon location – away from a regular path, for example – and its exact location is uploaded to the internet (www.geocaching.com or, more UK-specific but less well known, www.opencaching.org.uk – see Chapter 10) so that others may then discover it using a hand-held GPS device and a little ingenuity. Traditional caches such as these usually contain a logbook and pencil to enable finders to record their discovery, which they later also put on the website.

## THE HISTORY OF GEOCACHING

The modern leisure pursuit of geocaching (pronounced 'gee-o-cash-ing') became a possibility only when what is known as 'selective availability' – a policy adopted by the US Department of Defense to introduce some intentional 'noise' into their Global Positioning System (GPS) satellite signals in order to degrade their accuracy for civilian users – was removed from civilian GPS devices in 2000 (see Chapter 2). Until then, GPS units (other than those used for military purposes) were neither precise nor useful. Suddenly, with a GPS device it became possible to pinpoint, very accurately, any given location using co-ordinates of both latitude and longitude. Once that became achievable it was just one short step for outdoor mankind into the world of high-tech treasure hunting.

Geocaching owes a lot to both the traditional forms of treasure hunting and letterboxing (a treasure hunt that required you to decipher clues left in landmarks and printed materials). Today, geocaching uses technology and often (but not always) a series of clues to locate a position, or 'cache', or other piece of information.

Jack (The Magna Defender) finds Fozzie Bear (GC103JQ)

There are 'rules' covering the contents of caches, and items are required to be safe and suitable for all ages. If a cache is reported to contain questionable items, it can be temporarily disabled by a reviewer until the offending items are removed.

On 3 May 2000, an Oregon resident planted the first geocache. He posted the GPS location on a Usenet group, and it was found twice within three days. Geocaching was born, and the rest, as they say, is history.

In the UK, Hampshire County Council was the first local authority, and major landowner, in the UK to officially recognise geocaching as a great way of getting families and others out into the countryside, and as a valuable educational resource. In July 2003, Hampshire County Council, with members of the geocaching community, held the first organised geocaching event in the UK to be officially recognised by any major landowner and opened to members of the non-geocaching community. It took place at Farley Mount Country Park.

## IS IT FOR YOU?

Geocaching is great for anyone who loves sightseeing and leisure activities in the outdoors, and for those who, perhaps for health reasons, are looking for an enjoyable way to get some fresh air and exercise. It gives you an excuse to go off the beaten path and take notice of what's around you – things that you might otherwise would take for granted.

And geocaching is a pursuit that can be followed by all ages, from young children to those enjoying their retirement years.

Geocaching will also appeal to anyone who likes puzzles and challenges, because not all the cache information is readily given. You may find that you need to visit more than one location in order to acquire information that feeds into final co-ordinates, and/or that the information comes in the guise of cryptic (sometimes very cryptic) clues.

It also helps if you have a streak of the explorer or pirate in you. Searching for treasure is what it's all about. Some people look on geocaching as playing with high-tech toys; in fact it's rather more of an adventure. You may have sophisticated tools at your disposal, but finding a geocache takes wits, know-how and patience. Geocaching is not like a board game where you can rely on strategies and chance. Instead you need to be able to decipher clues left by those who hide the cache, and you must travel to the hidden cache as well. This requires time and can demand a reasonable level of physical fitness.

**Five-baa-ed gate – when geocaching in rural areas, always observe the Countryside Code (see Appendix C) (photo: Mark Fishwick)**

## USING THE GEOCACHING WEBSITE

The principal key to geocaching is a website – www.geocaching.com – owned and managed by a business called Groundspeak, which is based in the US. So to take part in geocaching you need to have access to a computer with a web browser, and to be moderately competent at using both.

The first thing to do is to register on the website and then 'invent' a name for yourself. There's nothing to stop you using your personal name – unless someone else has already used the same name. But there is fun in devising a pseudonym under which you play the game. Take a look at some of the logs entered on the website to get the idea.

On the website you'll find information that tells you where there are geocaches in your locality, or indeed worldwide. You'll be surprised to find that you probably pass some on a daily basis.

Once you've found the information about geocaches you need to obtain co-ordinates from the website for each individual cache, which will tell you fairly precisely where the cache is hidden. Then all you have to do is go out and find it. When you get to the location, the cache won't be instantly obvious; most are well hidden and need to be searched for. But the search is all part of the fun, and all the more so because it's something that (according to geocaching 'rules') must be done away from prying eyes – in other words, do not search for, retrieve or replace a cache if anyone who is not in your group can see you. In this way you minimise the risk of the cache being removed or damaged, leaving it in place for the next geocacher to find. And, as some of the caches are intentionally in popular and busy locations, this in itself is often quite difficult – sometimes impossible. Sadly, hardly a week goes by without some mention of caches having been 'muggled' (removed or destroyed by non-geocachers). So it's vitally important both to ensure you are not observed, and to replace the cache carefully, out of sight.

Having found a cache, enter your name in its logbook, along with the date, and then replace the cache. When you get home, record your find and write a few notes on the geocaching website. The website is remarkably ingenious and tots up your personal finds, keeping a life-long record of your geocaching activity.

Of course, there are times when you may not find your chosen geocache. Perhaps your search wasn't diligent enough, or the cache was found by a 'muggle', or perhaps a fox that knocked it about a bit, thinking there may be food in

A historical cache location on the Isle of Mull – locations that have a history and a story to tell are always popular

it. Then you need to record on the website the fact that you did not find it (DNF) to enable the 'owner' to investigate.

## WHAT YOU NEED TO GET STARTED

The website gives co-ordinate information for caches in two forms: latitude and longitude; or a reference point from the British grid system. (Of course, if you visit countries outside the UK the grid system is not applicable.) In order to use the co-ordinate information you need a GPS device, a small hand-held instrument that uses satellite technology to locate your position, rather like a SatNav in a car. You can store cache co-ordinates on GPS devices and then use the device to locate them. Using a GPS is not difficult, but neither is it intuitive – although a little practice goes a long way. When you arrive at your location, all you have to do is find the cache.

If you're adept at using a map and compass, then you don't even need a GPS – not in the UK at least – as the grid references are accurate enough to pinpoint the locality of the cache on a map. But, it has to be said, a GPS device can get you closer to your target than using grid references for the simple reason that the satellite system relays your position fairly accurately (using numerous satellite points of

The Wheel Stones EarthCache on Derwent Edge: many EarthCaches require a photograph to give evidence of your visit

reference) and tells you when you arrive at the cache location, whereas using map and compass to achieve the same thing uses only two points of reference (northings and eastings), which requires a much higher degree of navigational skill.

So, all you need is a GPS device (see Chapter 2) and a basic understanding of the use of the internet... and off you go. Increasingly, software apps are available to run the geocaching system on mobile phones and tablet devices. They're increasingly accurate, and can be adequate for anyone who wants to experiment before committing to the expenditure of a GPS device. Of course, none of this means you should discard map and compass – they will still come in handy, if only to find your way around fields or across rivers.

As geocaching is an outdoor pursuit, it follows that you'll need adequate outdoor clothing, and a decent pair of walking boots, if you plan to seek out the more remote caches. There are caches on the summits of mountains, in caves, under bridges, beside rivers, deep in woodland cover and along canals – in fact, you may encounter all kinds of terrain, and need to be suitably equipped.

## THE BASIC RULES OF GEOCACHING

As with any 'game', there are rules, but in the case of geocaching they are few and uncomplicated.

- Having successfully arrived at the approximate location of the cache, it is important that you do not look for it, retrieve it or replace it if you can be observed by non-geocachers (muggles).
- Sign the logbook with the date and your geocaching pseudonym. If the logbook is large enough, you may want to add a comment. If you're the first person to find the cache, you should also enter the time.
- If you wish to, feel free to take items from the cache (always exchange them for something of equal or greater value, unless they are items designed specifically to be taken and moved on), although some caches are too small to accommodate anything other than the log.
- Replace the cache exactly where you found it and conceal it appropriately. If you move the cache to a slightly different location, even if the co-ordinates are the same, you may have lessened the challenge for others and taken some of the fun out of it. Conversely, do not replace the cache in such a way that it becomes virtually impossible to find or retrieve.

**Popular geographical locations are ideal places to conceal and look for caches – and avoiding muggles is part of the fun (photo: Mark Fishwick)**

SYMONDS YAT

HEIGHT ABOVE SEA LEVEL 504

Not all geocaches are easily accessible; for some you need to put in the effort to reach locations like Seathwaite Tarn in Cumbria

# 2 GPS DEVICES

Before you can take part in your first search for a geocache you need some basic tools. Although, as mentioned in the previous chapter, you can theoretically manage without it for some geocaches (or use a mobile phone app), ultimately you really need a GPS device, along with the co-ordinates of the cache you are looking for. You'll also need a map of the area, and perhaps a compass too, although most GPS devices have an in-built compass.

For aeons, man has looked to the sky to calculate his whereabouts; traditionally, the sun and the fixed stars have been our guides. But today, constellations of man-made satellites have taken over as signals to guide our way.

## THE GLOBAL POSITIONING SYSTEM (GPS) EXPLAINED

GPS satellites, powered by solar energy, orbit the Earth about twice a day, travelling at approximately 11,000 miles above the planet and at some 7000mph (see diagram below). They were designed as a navigational system for military operations, but are now increasingly used for other

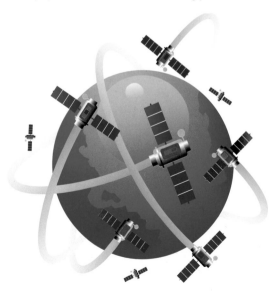

activities. Each satellite sends out a unique radio signal, and a GPS device on Earth can take readings and measurements from up to 24 satellites. It uses these to compute the distance to the satellite and so work out the location of the GPS. It's rare to get pinpoint accuracy, but for the purposes of geocaching this is not wholly necessary, as part of the fun is the 'hunt' once you get close.

The satellites are in such orbits that at any one time your GPS device can pick up signals from at least six, and often more, varying over time as satellites come in and out of 'view'. A display on the GPS shows how many satellites your device is connecting with; you need contact with at least four satellites to get a clear 3-D fix on location and altitude. Fewer than this and you get only a 2-D fix, but this, in general, is not a critical issue for geocaching – unless you're seeking caches concealed on mountain summits.

For many years, the US (GPS) and, later, Russia (Glonass) provided the only global satellite navigation systems available. A third system, the EU's Galileo, became fully functioning in 2013. The three systems are completely integrated, which means you are able to determine a position by picking up signals from any combination of satellites belonging to any of the three systems.

Anyone can use the satellite system – it's completely free. The system has long been used by aircraft and shipping, but is increasingly being used by surveyors, map-makers, conservationists, mobile phone networks, emergency services, walkers and motorists.

## SELECTING A GPS DEVICE

Although it is possible to spend a significant fortune on the most sophisticated GPS device, accurate in certain conditions to 1cm, such expense or accuracy is not necessary for geocaching. If your GPS receiver deposits you within 1cm of a cache, some of the fun is taken away from the experience. Searching for the concealed cache is part of the game, so something a bit more modest is perfectly acceptable.

But one thing is of key importance: no one device is significantly more accurate than another. So you can buy the cheapest and still enjoy the experiences of geocaching. Some of the more sophisticated ones, however, have additional features and are geocaching-specific – that is, they're *designed* for geocaching and have added features to enable you to store large numbers of cache co-ordinates and to record finds.

It's important to realise that a GPS device will direct you to the cache co-ordinates by the most direct route – a straight line – and this may be far from achievable, since the

GPS takes no account of intervening rivers, valleys, mountains, forests, farm fields and sundry other obstructions. The GPS will point you in the right direction, but you need to figure out for yourself how to get there. This is where a map and compass, and the ability to use both, comes in useful. Quite often you won't need a map and compass, but equally often you will, not least to ensure that you avoid trespassing.

In the UK, the principal supplier of GPS devices is Garmin, and they have a wide range of instruments.

**Garmin GPS devices**

All GPS devices offer the same functionality, so any variation in price is entirely dependent on additional built-in features. Understanding your needs will help determine how you spend your money, although there is much to be said for acquiring a basic device first and then upgrading at some later stage once you have an idea of how the additional features (and expenditure) might best serve you. Considerations you might want to take into account are:

- do I need my GPS to display maps?
- how much more helpful would it be to have a device that is geocaching compatible?
- do I want the GPS to hold all relevant information about the cache (paperless caching), or can I manage with just the essentials?
- in what type of terrain am I most likely to be using the GPS?
- is size and weight of any concern?
- what can I afford?

**A word about geocaching compatibility**
Basic GPS devices are not geocaching compatible; more sophisticated devices are. The latter will store your co-ordinate information in a special 'Geocaching' folder, from which you can select your caches on the trail. It lists these caches in the order of those nearest to you, in a straight line.

Once you've located the cache, you can tell the device that you've done so and it will direct you to the next nearest cache without your having to scroll through the database. It can even be programmed to add your daily finds to the in-built calendar for later referencing, although these entries will be simultaneously removed once you delete the cache record from the device. The most sophisticated GPS devices and smartphone apps (see below) will also allow you to log your find directly to the website.

There is another difference between basic and sophisticated devices: most cache codes (the arrangement of numbers and letters, beginning with 'GC', that identifies the cache) consist of seven characters. Basic devices store only the first six of these, whereas more expensive devices store them all. The significance of this becomes apparent if you're following a series of caches placed by the same owner, all of which begin with the same first six characters (with only the final character being different). A basic device will store only one of the caches, and if you try to send other similar codes to the device it will simply overwrite the earlier entries, so instead of having a series of caches in your GPS you will have only one. Devices that are geocaching compatible do not have this problem and will download all the codes in full.

## IPHONES, BLACKBERRIES AND ANDROIDS

Before you rush out and buy a GPS device, you might want to pause – especially if you own an iPhone, BlackBerry or Android smartphone. All these devices are capable of downloading and operating geocaching software that works every bit as efficiently as a conventional GPS device. These applications use mobile broadband (4G, 3G or GPRS) to download information and are amazingly accurate. The software is not free, but is considerably cheaper than buying a new GPS device. However, you first need to check that your smartphone has GPS capability, and that this is activated on your account.

Where these applications score over conventional GPS devices is in offering additional functions, such as:
- search by current location, address or cache code
- filter your own hides and finds from the www.geocaching.com search results
- access geocache details, including description, photo gallery, attributes, recent logs, hint and inventory
- look up trackable item details, including item goals, while on the trail (see Chapter 8)
- save geocache listings, including maps and photos, for quick retrieval and offline use

- log geocache finds and post notes or logs in the field
- download active Pocket Queries (see Chapter 9) for use while outside of network coverage
- view geocache web pages on www.geocaching.com without leaving the application, using embedded web browser.

There are also advanced capabilities, which allow the user to:
- view nearby caches on the embedded map
- view cache size, terrain and difficulty rating directly from the map screen
- navigate to geocaches with a simulated compass arrow, or directly from the map screen
- add custom waypoints when navigating to multi-caches
- switch between street, topographic and satellite maps.

Many of these features are included as standard in top-end conventional GPS devices. Of course, these particular applications are changing all the time, but the beauty of a mobile phone application is in the ability it provides

**Displays of the iPhone geocaching application**

**Display of Memory Map Adventurer 2800**

**Displays from Navigator Trimble on BlackBerry**

**The SatMap Active 12 GPS device**

The glaciated mountains of Cadair Idris in the Snowdonia National Park provide another great location for an EarthCache

– should you be away from your normal base, perhaps unexpectedly – to search for nearby caches to fill a spare moment.

Geocaching options also feature on other GPS devices, such as the SatMap Active 10 and 12 and Memory Map devices, which are primarily map-based tracking systems, but with geocaching options built in.

## ACCURACY AND LIMITATIONS OF GPS DEVICES

For all practical purposes, GPS devices are not affected by weather conditions or cloud cover. But to get an accurate and clear reading, GPS devices (and this includes the mobile phone applications) require a clear view of the sky in order to pick up satellite signals. Reception, and therefore accuracy, can be affected by woodland cover, the nearby presence of cliffs or tall buildings.

There are five main factors affecting GPS accuracy:

* The position of the satellites at any given time: so-called **ephemeris errors** occur when the satellite does not correctly transmit its exact position in orbit.
* **Conditions in the Earth's upper atmosphere** can affect transmissions from the satellites.
* **Timing errors** are possible because, while the satellites each have an atomic clock (accurate to within three nanoseconds or three-billionths of a second), the clock in your GPS device is significantly less accurate, and this can cause slight positional inconsistencies.
* **Multi-path errors** occur when a satellite signal bounces off a hard surface – such as a building or a cliff – before it reaches the receiver, causing a time delay and an inaccurate calculation of distance.
* **Poor satellite coverage** can occur when you do not have a wide and open view of the sky (which makes geocaching in cities much more difficult than in more open spaces).

No matter how expensive and sophisticated the GPS device you choose, if the cache owner used a basic device to calculate the co-ordinates, no amount of high-tech gadgetry is going to make your readings any more accurate. Think before you spend!

**2**

GPS DEVICES

### GPS MEMORY

GPS devices have differing amounts of internal memory, and this will determine the number of waypoints, logs, routes and geocaching data you can store. Unlike iPhones, Blackberries and personal computers, you cannot add new memory chips to a GPS device. Some of the more expensive devices, however, are capable of accepting memory cards on which data and maps can be stored.

A GPS device is an electronic instrument and it therefore relies on battery power. These can (and do) run down, so it is essential to carry spares at all times. Moreover, the instrument can be damaged or it can simply malfunction. Most of the dedicated GPS receivers are waterproof, but the same may not be true of mobile phone receivers.

## USING A GPS RECEIVER

Left to its own devices, as soon as you switch on a GPS it will begin searching for satellites with which to communicate. But before this can be of meaningful use to you, it is necessary to complete a small set-up procedure, beginning with initialisation.

You first need to get a fix on your current position. To do this, take the device outdoors into a large open area away from buildings and trees. Turn the device on and keep it face-up and parallel with the ground. If this is the first time you've used the device, it will perform a self-test, which is then followed by a satellite page informing you that it's searching for satellites. The device needs to receive strong signals from at least three satellites for it to be able to find your position. When it has done so, you'll see a 'Ready to navigate' message, and you are now ready to go. However, when you use the device for the first time it can take up to five minutes to find your location; thereafter this should be only a matter of 15–30 seconds. This is because each satellite transmits its own orbital data, known as an 'almanac', every 30 seconds. If the device is left off for some time the information becomes dated, and so it can take a few moments to update itself.

You may also need to complete a small set-up routine, just to ensure that the device is functioning correctly for your location. The 'Set-up' screens are under the 'Menu' page, but devices may differ in this regard. Some of the options are obvious, such as time and date. You should set these accordingly. The only option that is of real concern is on the page called 'Units' – again this may differ from device to device. There are only three entries you need concern yourself with initially: the first is 'Position format', which relates to the form in which co-ordinate information is relayed to you. For geocaching this needs to be set at hddd*mm. mmm (degrees and decimal minutes – see 'A question of degree' box, below). You also need to set the Map Datum to WGS84 (see 'Understanding co-ordinate systems', below).

Lastly, it is your preference whether the units are expressed as metric or statute – it's just a question of whether you want kilometres and metres or miles and feet. The significance of the position format and datum are explained below.

## UNDERSTANDING CO-ORDINATE SYSTEMS

A co-ordinate system is simply a way of describing locations on a map. Across the different countries of the world there are many co-ordinate systems. The British Ordnance Survey, for example, has the grid system – a network of pale blue lines over-printed on maps. This works well because Britain is comparatively small. But in larger countries the curvature of the Earth makes the accuracy of a two-dimensional plan superimposed on what is really a three-dimensional object (the Earth) rather poor. So there are few countries that use this form of grid system. For geocaching purposes it's simpler to use latitude and longitude, the oldest of the map co-ordinate systems.

### A NETWORK OF LINES

Lines of **latitude** run horizontally around the Earth, parallel to the equator (think 'lat' = 'flat', or latitude = around the Earth). These lines measure distances north or south of the equator, and will be your north/south co-ordinates.

As you go north or south from the equator, so the latitude increases from 0° to 90° as you arrive at the poles.

Lines of **longitude** run vertically up the Earth, connecting the north and south poles (think 'long' = 'long lines', or longitude = over the poles). These lines measure the distance, east or west, of the prime meridian at Greenwich in London, England, and these will be your east/west co-ordinates.

When you travel east or west from the prime meridian, the longitude increases from 0° to 180°. The place where the two 180° lines of longitude meet (roughly in the middle of the Pacific Ocean) is known as the International Date Line.

If you're simply out for a walk in the British countryside, then the OS grid system is perfectly adequate; a six-figure grid reference is sufficient to show a location on a map, and with appropriate map-reading skills you can use map and compass to walk to that location. But for the purposes of geocaching it's generally accepted that the use of latitude and longitude is the norm, and this is the principal system used on www.geocaching.com. It is also the system needed if you are geocaching outside the UK.

## A QUESTION OF DEGREE

Geocaching co-ordinates are presented in the format hddd*mm.mmm, where 'h' is a letter indicating 'N'orth, 'S'outh, 'E'ast or 'W'est. In the UK everything is 'N' (north of the equator) or 'E' or 'W' of the Greenwich meridian. 'ddd' represents the degrees (north, east or west), while 'mm.mmm' represents decimal minutes to three points.

One degree of latitude is a significant distance, around 70 miles. However, one degree of longitude decreases to zero miles as you head north or south from the equator to the poles. In the UK it ranges from 35 to 44 miles.

A degree is composed of 60 minutes, so a minute of latitude is about 1.2 miles, and a minute of longitude 0.6–0.7 miles.

If all that seems confusing, then you can totally ignore it. All you need to understand is that by this system you can pinpoint a particular location very accurately. Co-ordinates, expressed as numbers, will look like this –

N    53°    42.660
W    002°   38.914

– which is one of the author's caches. This is expressed in degrees and decimal minutes. But over the years, other formats have been devised using either degrees, minutes and seconds (N 53° 42′39″ W 002° 38′54″) or decimal degrees (N 53.7110 W 002.6486). All three sets of co-ordinates are for the same cache, which shows how confusing things can become, and why it's important to set your GPS device to hddd*mm.mmm, which is what all geocachers use. (The three sets of co-ordinates given above differ because: in the first set the minutes are decimalised; in the third set the degrees are decimalised; and the second set doesn't decimalise anything.)

For basic cache searches you don't need to understand the significance of this information, nor do you need the alternative formats. But for some more complicated caches you need to understand degrees and decimal minutes well enough to be able to input the data for yourself.

## UNDERSTANDING DATUMS

For reasons that are complex and confusing to a layperson, there is no one agreed latitude and longitude co-ordinate system. There are many different meridians of zero longitude (prime meridians) and circles of zero latitude (equators), although the former generally pass somewhere near Greenwich and the latter is always somewhere near the rotational equator. Different countries base their maps on different mathematical models and on projections representing the shape of the Earth's surface, which, contrary to popular belief, is not a perfect orb but an ellipsoid (flattened at the poles). Each different model is known as a map datum, and many of the world's datums are already programmed into GPS devices.

The result of this mish-mash of information is that different systems of latitude and longitude can disagree on the co-ordinates of any given point by more than 200m. For any application where an error of this size would be significant – docking with a space station, for example – it's important to know which system is being used and exactly how it is defined. Fortunately, for geocaching purposes, the system is simplified; everyone uses the World Geodetic System 1984, known as WGS84, and this is the datum you should select when setting up your GPS device. Should you subsequently want to switch to using the British grid system, then you will need to change the datum to British Grid.

Detailed (and complex) explanations of modern GPS systems are available on the www.ordnancesurvey.co.uk website.

**Geocaches are often in remote locations, calling for hill-walking experience, as here at the Salt Cellar, Derwent Edges, Peak District (photo: Jon Young)**

The hedgerow margins along Britain's farm fields make perfect locations for geocaches

# 3 GETTING STARTED

The beauty of geocaching is that, compared to many other leisure pursuits, it need not be inordinately expensive. Of course, to start you do need certain basic items of equipment – not least a GPS receiver. You could manage without a GPS, but your scope for finding caches will be limited and the process more time-consuming, and unless you're exceptionally gifted at navigation with map and compass it is more satisfying to invest in a GPS device.

The basic items you need, then, are your GPS device, a map of the area you're in, and the co-ordinates of the caches you're searching for. Chapter 2 deals with various aspects of GPS devices and software for use on an iPhone or BlackBerry. There are advantages and disadvantages to each, but it's a good idea to start with an inexpensive GPS device, get the hang of what you're doing, and then decide whether you need to buy something more up-market or investigate how to use your mobile phone for geocaching.

## USING WWW.GEOCACHING.COM

The key website to geocaching is www.geocaching.com. Although there are other websites that provide cache co-ordinates (such as www.opencaching.org.uk – see Chapter 10), www.geocaching.com is the founding website.

When you first connect with the website it looks a little bewildering, but the more you use it, the clearer things become. The layout of the website may change in future years, but it will contain all the same essential information. What is immediately obvious is that it is very much US-oriented, so you need to allow for this. The site www.opencaching.org.uk gets round this issue, but has very few caches in its database at the time of writing (April 2014).

## CREATING A MEMBERSHIP

The first thing you need to do is to create a membership.

There are two levels of membership: basic, and premium. Basic membership is free; premium membership has a fairly nominal subscription. At first you may not understand the significance of the differences between the two levels of membership, but suffice to say that the basic

**Screenshot of www.geocaching.com home page**

membership is just that – basic – allowing you to download co-ordinates and location information for caches and to share your experiences online. This is all you need in order to make a start, so it is advisable to opt for this level of membership initially.

However, it will soon become apparent that this option is very limited, and you will find yourself opting for premium membership. Be aware that some caches are available only to premium members, so if you elect to have basic membership you will not have access to all the caches.

More information about the benefits of premium membership is given in Chapter 9.

To create an account for yourself, and effect membership registration, select either 'Create account' from the top right of the screen, or 'Join' in the top menu bar. Both options take you to a Membership Registration page, the details of which are self-explanatory, and enable you to make a start.

### Make a name for yourself

Part of the process of creating a membership is deciding on a 'name' for yourself. All the obvious ones – cachebuster, cachemaster, cache machine, cache register, and so on – have long since gone. So you need to invent a pseudonym for yourself that is, perhaps, a composite of initials or names, such as PamandFred, Meandthedog,

LostnWet, or something that has significance to you. The author uses 'countrymatters' because, in addition to being a writer of guidebooks about geocaching, he is also a travel journalist to whom countries matter, and an outdoor writer and photographer for whom the country[side] matters. You get the drift? And, yes, he does know to what Shakespeare was referring in Hamlet when he mentions 'country matters'.

If you subsequently decide that you want to change your geocaching pseudonym, you can contact Groundspeak and ask for your name to be changed. This will automatically be transferred to all your log entries, all your finds and all your own caches.

### Validation

Having devised a name and created a membership, you're almost ready to go. Part of the membership creation process requires you to validate the email address you're using. So, once you've selected your pseudonym and agreed to the terms and conditions under which geocaching operates, you will be sent an email asking you to validate that the email address really is yours. Once this is done, you can then log in to www.geocaching.com.

### Adding your home co-ordinates

Once you've created your membership it's a wise move to add your home co-ordinates. This enables the website database to send you information about caches near you.

Calculating your home co-ordinates can be done either by using your GPS device – it's a good idea to do this outside your home, assuming it's not surrounded by high-rise buildings that will obstruct a satellite signal – or by asking the website to do it for you:

- Log in to the website and select 'Your profile' (top menu).
- From the drop-down menu select 'Quick view'. At first you have an almost blank profile screen, but on the right is a small panel headed 'Search options', with a message saying 'You have not set a home location'. This is followed by the option to 'Add them now'.
- Select 'Add them now' and you are taken through to a screen showing a map headed 'Manage location'.
- Try entering your postcode (including the space) into the 'Search' field, and click on the 'Search' button. If your postcode does not conflict with a similar code in another country, you are then taken through to another map with a small panel on it pointing to a man icon

at your postcode location. However, because UK post-codes cover more than one property, the icon may not correspond exactly with your home address. For complete accuracy simply drag the icon to the correct position on the map, and make a note of the latitude and longitude co-ordinates now showing both on the icon and in the 'Search' field above it.

- Select 'Save changes'. You have now told the website where you are.

## UNDERSTANDING CACHE PAGES

On the 'Your profile' page, under 'Search Options' (right-hand menu), you'll find 'Search for geocaches' near your home location. Click on this, or the nearby map icon, and this will take you to a page showing 'All geocaches' near your home. Select one of the caches from the list and click on its name to be taken to the detailed 'Cache page'. The screenshots on the following pages show the top and bottom of a typical cache page. There's a lot of information on cache pages, so it's worth ensuring that you understand it. Much of the information is also in the table that you get when you search the website for geocaches (see 'Querying the database' below), but there is so much more detail here, and it is this page with which you need to become familiar.

### Geocache code and name

A unique 'GC' code (automatically generated by the website) for each cache is shown at the top right of the cache page – GC33YA1 in this case. The name – 'Mull: Lochan na Guailne Duibhe' – appears in bold type at the top centre of the page. To the left of the name appears an icon that tells you what type of cache it is (see Chapter 4 for more information about the different types of cache).

### Cache owner

The name of the person who placed the cache, known as the 'owner', appears immediately below the name of the cache, alongside the date on which it was hidden. The name is a pseudonym – in other words, the owner's www. geocaching.com username. If you click on the name, in this case 'countrymatters', you are taken to a page that gives more information about the cache owner. This is their profile page; you will have a similar page, which you can edit.

### Calendar option

If the cache relates to an event, the cache page will show an additional element immediately below the name of the cache at the top of the page. This is 'Add to Calendar', a

An example of a cache page (top half)

neat device that, when selected, puts the event details into whatever form of calendar your computer is using (Google, Outlook, Windows Live or Yahoo, for example).

## Difficulty and Terrain (D/T)

Immediately below the cache owner's name are two indicators that tell you about the 'difficulty' you might experience in finding the cache, and the nature and condition of the 'terrain' you will encounter. In this context, 1 is easiest and 5 is the hardest, and the grades are subdivided into halves. This information is often presented together, in the form '1/1' (difficulty/terrain) – this example would therefore be presented as 3/3. In total there are 81 possible combinations (more is explained in Chapter 10 about 'D/T grids') and for many geocachers it becomes a challenge in itself to find caches of every level. However, while the 'terrain' grade is a fairly clear indicator of what to expect, the 'difficulty' grade may refer either to the actual difficulty of spotting and retrieving the cache, or to the fact that you may have to solve a complex puzzle in order to discover the co-ordinates. Grading is entirely subjective (see also Chapter 7) and the cache creator designates the level.

**Additional Waypoints** (Add / Edit waypoints)
No additional waypoints to display.

**Find...**

- ...other caches hidden or found by this user
- ...nearby caches of this type, that I haven't found
- ...all nearby caches, that I haven't found
- ...all nearby waymarks on Waymarking.com

**For online maps...**

- Geocaching.com Map
- Streetmap.co.uk
- Google Maps
- MapQuest
- Yahoo Maps
- Bing Maps
- OpenCycleMap
- OpenStreetMap

View Larger Map

500 m
1000 ft

About our maps

Notes about Printing Maps

**299 Logged Visits**

😃 293   😄 4   📷 1   🔦 1

Decrypt ↻

View Logbook | View the Image Gallery of 22 images

**Warning! Spoilers may be included in the descriptions or links.

---

**Nik&Erry**
☆ Premium Member

😃 92

😃 **Found it**                                                    03/09/2014

What a beautiful site. I have half muggle Nic and Sir Barkley Malcolm the trackable dog with me, everyone said a respectful hello to the fairies before finding the cache then taking some pictures. Thanks for bringing us here. TFTC

This entry was edited by Nik&Erry on Monday, 10 March 2014 at 22:31:04 UTC.

View Log

---

**ItsSpitting**
☆ Premium Member

😃 748

😃 **Found it**                                                    02/16/2014

Here for a week of geocaching on Skye. Glorious day, said hello to the fairies and asked they might help us have a successful caching trip. TB's visited. TFTC.

View Log

---

**Rich_Connie**
☆ Member

😃 59

😃 **Found it**                                                    12/02/2013

Found it and got soaked on a very rainy day :) I said hello to the fairies as I wanted to keep them on side.

View Log

---

**FMC1066**
☆ Premium Member

😃 740

😃 **Found it**                                                    11/01/2013

Found in the rain on the last day of our holiday to Skye.
Tftc

View Log

---

**An example of a cache page (bottom half)**

## Cache size

Next to the D/T information a small grey panel gives an indication of the size of cache container you're looking for. The options are 'micro', 'small', 'regular', 'large' and 'other'. The last category may be accompanied by further details in the information section below. There is a subdivision of 'micro', which may appear only in the cache description, and this is 'nano'. Nanos are very small and very hard to spot – they tend to be black or camouflage-coloured, and magnetic.

For many years, it was the norm to have cache containers that were 'regular' in size – Tupperware boxes and the like. Then, as the activity developed, a range of purpose-made cache containers appeared, among which were some that were very small, some well camouflaged, and some very devious. But they all made the pursuit all the more enjoyable.

## Favourites

Introduced in 2012, the 'Favourites' option allows you to award a point to any particular cache that you found especially appealing. The way to do this is detailed below (page 78). But the incidence of Favourite Points is an indicator of particularly popular caches, for any one of a number of reasons.

## Cache co-ordinates

Moving down the cache page, you reach a panel giving location information. This is in three parts:

- the first is the latitude and longitude co-ordinates
- the second is the same information expressed in the British grid format
- the third tells you how far the cache is located from your home co-ordinates.

It's important to remember that latitude and longitude use the WGS84 datum (see Chapter 2), while the British grid datum uses, as the name implies, the British Grid system. You can use either, but must ensure that your GPS receiver is set to the appropriate datum.

Select the link to 'Other conversions' and you'll find the cache co-ordinates expressed in other formats. In the UK, geocachers use degrees and decimal minutes, so these other conversions have little relevance (unless you're also using a car SatNav device to get to a driveable cache location).

**A group of friends enjoying a geocaching walk across Morecambe Bay**

### Printed information

The next option on the cache page is to print a copy of the cache page information, with a choice to include no log entries made by other finders, or five or ten logs. You can even ask the website to give you information about how you can drive from your home co-ordinates to the cache. However, while this may be useful in some situations, it does need treating with a measure of caution, since it is not possible to drive to many cache locations (because they are up mountains or in the middle of fields, for example). Moreover, you're likely to know your own locality better than www.geocaching.com. So use this option as a guide, but no more. Cache locations to which you can drive and park momentarily, while you retrieve the cache, are known as 'drive-by' caches or 'cache and dash'.

### Co-ordinate downloads: 'Send to GPS'

With the exception of low-end GPS devices, it is possible to use an interface cable that allows you to connect your GPS to your computer and directly download co-ordinate information. Called 'paperless geocaching', this works especially well with geocaching-friendly GPS devices, which also allow you to download associated co-ordinates, such as the location of convenient car parks or relevant landmarks. To use this option, you will need to have downloaded software called **Garmin Communicator**, which is simply the means by which the website can 'talk' to your GPS device. The software is downloaded from www8.garmin.com/products/communicator, and comes in PC and Mac versions. Of course, in the UK this works only with Garmin devices, and is not supported by all browsers.

Once the software is installed on your computer, simply connect your GPS device and click on 'Send to GPS'. This opens the Garmin Communicator, on which you will need to select the brand name of your device (Garmin, for example – there are others), following which the system writes the cache information to your GPS device, ready for you to retrieve.

Using what's known as a 'Pocket Query' and additional (free) software, it's possible to bulk-download cache information to your GPSr (see Chapter 9).

### Personal cache note

Below the section for downloading co-ordinates to your GPS is a pink field into which you can enter a personal note about the cache. No-one else can see your note. This is a useful provision, especially for puzzle caches, because you can enter the co-ordinates, once you've solved the puzzle, for future reference. You may also have picked up information about this particular cache from other geocachers or from reading earlier logs, and, again, it's useful to enter the information here.

## Geocache description

Cache descriptions range from brief notes to quite extended descriptions of the cache locality, local history, the geology and geography of the surrounding countryside, and the environment in which the cache is located. Often there are clues within the description, so it's important to read all the information carefully.

In some instances there may be specific instructions on how to approach the cache location (generally referred to as the 'GZ' or Ground Zero); these may be (a) practical, or (b) provided in order to avoid difficult or sensitive areas. It's important to observe any requirements of this nature, since failure to comply could result in permission to maintain the cache being withdrawn by the landowner.

Some cache descriptions also include images, artwork or code, and, quite often, a note about satellite reception if it is particularly variable at the cache location.

## Additional hints

The cache page itself is a rich source of information and may include an encrypted hint from the cache owner (although not all caches have or need them). Previous finders may have uploaded photos or included clues in their online log. Be careful, though: too much information may inadvertently ruin the fun for you.

The encrypted hints use a simple code format known as the half-reversed alphabet (ROT13), which looks like this:

A  B  C  D  E  F  G  H  I  J  K  L  M
N  O  P  Q  R  S  T  U  V  W  X  Y  Z

It's easy enough to decipher as it involves simple transposition (reading either up or down to find the corresponding letter). The word GEOCACHE, for example, translates as TRBPNPUR. But www.geocaching.com has a decryption option anyway; all you need to do is click on 'Decrypt' and it is done instantly.

However, you have to make a decision about these clues. Do you use them, or not? They usually give very clear guidance on where to locate the cache, such as 'under a fence' or 'next to an old pipe'. Do you want that level of information, or do you want to try without it first? Only you can decide, but it's worth remembering that some caches would never be found without the clue, and, to be honest, even with the clue some remain elusive.

GETTING STARTED

On your first geocaching expeditions you may want to keep a notebook in which you write down the code and name of the cache(s) you're looking for, along with the clue – deciphered or not, according to what you decide. You can always leave the clue encoded, and then decipher it only if you need to.

Some caches are in very remote locations, where you need to be fully equipped and prepared for all weather and terrain conditions

## Additional waypoints

Under the section headed 'Additional waypoints' you may find information about where to park, about waypoints that will guide you to the cache location, or about other way-points that you must visit in order to gather all the information needed to help you to determine the cache co-ordinates. These will be downloaded automatically when you use the Garmin Communicator to write caches to your device.

## Find...

The 'Find' option has a number of links to:

- other caches placed or found by the same owner as the cache you're currently looking for
- nearby caches of the same type (such as traditional caches) that you have yet to find
- all nearby caches you have yet to find, regardless of type
- all waymarks listed on www.waymarking.com, about which there is more information in Chapter 10.

## For online maps...

If you're a premium member of www.geocaching.com, when you open a cache page on the website you'll find links to a number of online maps:

- Geocaching.com Map
- Google Maps
- Streetmap.co.uk
- MapQuest
- Yahoo Maps
- Bing Maps
- Open Cycle Maps
- Open Street Maps

**Typical Google map**

The most useful of these are the first three; the others are simply variations on a theme. So, let's take a look at these.

- A **Geocaching.com Map** shows not only the cache you were looking at, but all others nearby, making this the most useful tool for locating caches in any given area. This detailed map also uses different icons to denote the type of cache. With these maps you get an overview of a particular area, and can plan a campaign of cache retrieval based on this overview. Significantly, once you've logged online that you've found a cache, the icon on the map changes to a smiley face, thus avoiding your having to search for caches you've already found. Alongside the menu for online mapping is a section of a Google Map showing a cache icon just for the cache to which the page relates. Your own caches appear on this map as yellow stars.
- **Google Maps** provides a basic map of the area showing the approximate location of the cache, marked by a red symbol. This is not sufficient to get you close, but it will give you an idea of the direction and general area.
- **Streetmap.co.uk** shows the location of a cache identified by an arrow on an Ordnance Survey Landranger map. This gives you a good idea of the locality you need to get to, and is very useful in pre-planning.

GETTING STARTED

## Logged visits

The bottom part of the cache page is where you find other geocachers' log entries. These are briefly summarised in the box below.

 58 = found

 2 = not found

 2 = notes, posted by the cache owner, or other geocachers

 1 = the original entry/entries made by the cache reviewer (see Chapter 7)

More detailed log entries are then given, ranging from simple notes to extended entries detailing the experience of finding the cache. Some of the entries have images linked to them, which occasionally reveal information about the cache location. These are known as 'spoilers', for obvious reasons. Whether you use them or not is for you to decide.

## Navigation panel

At the top right of the cache page, below the cache code, is a small navigation panel. The panel contains just four elements, under 'Log your visit'. It is to this panel that you will ultimately return to log your find (see Chapter 6).

1. 'View gallery' allows you to view any images that have been uploaded for this particular cache.

2. 'Watch' enables you to mark this cache as something you want to monitor to see if anyone else finds it (usually if you've failed to do so yourself). It's also useful to use for 'Event caches' – see Chapter 4 – so that you can receive notifications about an event you hope to attend, and for which the event organiser might make changes/ announcements.

3. 'Bookmark' is a way of grouping (bookmarking) caches, the best caches in a given area, say, or of grouping together just those caches that you hope to search for on your next outing, rather than having to download a large number of caches to your GPS (which may have a memory limit).

4. 'Ignore' is an advanced option for caches that you may not want to show in any search results that you're generating.

The navigation panel also has an expanded view, available only to the cache owner, to enable editing of the cache page, amend attributes and so on.

## Map location of geocache

Below the Navigation panel is a small map showing the general area where the cache is located.

A larger map, containing more detail, appears as you scroll down the page. If you click on this larger map it takes you through to the Geocaching.com Map for the actual location, and also shows other nearby caches.

## Attributes

Under the map are symbols used to denote the cache's 'attributes', and these tell you what to expect at a cache location. Cache owners can assign attributes to their cache to indicate the following:

- **Permissions** – including whether dogs are allowed
- **Conditions** – whether there's a significant amount of walking involved on the route, its suitability for children, whether the cache is available at all times, and so on
- **Special equipment** – including parking fees, a torch or climbing equipment
- **Hazards** – such as thorns or dangerous terrain
- **Facilities** – including accessibility for wheelchairs, availability of parking and public transport.

Premium members can run a search, known as a Pocket Query (see Chapter 9), to search for caches with particular attributes – suitable for children, for example, or accessible to disabled people, and so on.

## Inventory

Chapter 8 gives more information about trackable items, known as Travel bugs or geocoins, that may be found in cache containers. Any such trackable items currently located in a cache are listed in the inventory (beneath the 'Attributes' list). However, it is worth bearing in mind that while the inventory shows trackable items that have been placed in the cache, they may in the meantime have been taken by another geocacher who has not yet had the opportunity to update the trackable log – this often happens with caches in and around tourist destinations.

## SEARCH OPTIONS: QUERYING THE DATABASE

The sensible thing to do first is to search for geocaches near your home.

On the home page of www.geocaching.com is a section headed 'Search for Nearby Geocaches'. In the data field immediately below, your home co-ordinates (assuming you have set them, as described above) will be displayed. Click on the small magnifying glass and the system will return a page of all the geocaches close to those co-ordinates. Entering your home postcode often yields the same information.

If your computer is using WiFi to connect to the internet, this search facility can be used to locate where you are (where you live). Just click on 'Find my location' and the system will do the rest, if it can, and will also generate co-ordinates for your home location, which will be saved in the field. However, this method is not wholly reliable.

You can also use this search field to insert the GC code for a particular cache, but as you have yet to find a cache this is something to come back to later.

You can also use this search option to find geocaches at any location. For example, enter 'Venice' and you get a list of all the caches in Venice. But if the place you search for has a US counterpart the answer will relate to that, and you'll need to refine your search.

Alternatively, you can enter your home postcode (with or without spaces), then click on 'Go', and you'll be presented with a list of caches near your home and radiating outwards from it for anything up to 40km (25 miles). You'll be surprised how many there are!

However, because of the US bias of the website, entering your postcode may not always work, particularly if there are identical or similar postcodes elsewhere in the world. If it doesn't work using your home postcode, try entering the name of a town near where you live. (Using the name of a village may not be sufficient, but major towns will be found.)

You can also reach cache information via the top drop-down menu: select 'Play' and then 'Hide and seek a cache', which allows you a greater choice of fields with which to narrow down your search. If you restrict your search criteria just to the UK, you'll find there are over 160,000 caches – reason enough to start narrowing things down. If you're fond of statistics, this information (and much more) is available at www.project-gc.com.

### Understanding the results

Once you have your list of caches you can start searching for them. All you do now is select the caches you want to go out and find. So, turn to the list you've generated; it will look something like the screenshot on page 45.

### But what does it all mean?

The first thing to realise is that the table is giving you information about caches concealed at a certain distance from your home co-ordinates. It helps if you can get a visual idea of where they are, and you can do this by selecting 'Map

## All Geocaches

N 53° 42.594 W 002° 38.581                    Map this Location | New Search

Total Records: **53868** - Page: **1** of **2694** -    < Prev  <<  <[1 2 3 4 5 6 7 8 9 10]>  >>  **Next >**

| □ | λ | ♀ | ☺ | Description | Info | (D / T) | Placed | Last Found | ↕ |
|---|---|---|---|---|---|---|---|---|---|
| □ | ↗ SW 0.24km | **1** | ☆ | **Cuerden Valley Park: Dead Wood** by countrymatters | GC1HVTF | Northwest England, United Kingdom | ⚲ | 2.5/2 | 11/04/2008 | 6 days ago* | |
| □ | ↖ SE 0.29km | | ☺ | **St Bedes secret** by Eavesy | GC3ORYF | Northwest England, United Kingdom | ⚲ | 1/1 | 10/16/2011 | 09/22/2013 01/04/2012 | |
| □ | ◄ W 0.39km | **5** | ☆ | **Cuerden Valley Park: Just so** by countrymatters | GC1WYMD | Northwest England, United Kingdom | | 3/2.5 | 08/07/2009 | 08/27/2013 | |
| □ | ▼ S 0.43km | | ☺ | **Shopaholics Paradise - Clayton Green** by The Magna Defender | GC4DH4P | Northwest England, United Kingdom | ◉ | 3/1.5 | 06/03/2013 | 4 days ago* 07/20/2013 | |
| □ | ↗ SW 0.53km | **5** | ☆ | **Cuerden Valley Park: Dead Good View** by countrymatters | GC1HXCQ | Northwest England, United Kingdom | ▯ | 2.5/3 | 11/06/2008 | 08/29/2013 | |
| □ | ▼ S 0.61km | | ☺ | **Sheep Hill Lane** by marc-fenix | GC348XG | Northwest England, United Kingdom | | 1.5/1.5 | 09/16/2011 | 3 days ago* 01/02/2012 | |
| □ | ↖ SE 0.62km | | ☺ | **The Beaver Bonus Cache part 1** by Squeezy Sue | GC1C5DG | United Kingdom | ⚲ | 1/1 | 05/11/2008 | 08/12/2013 10/23/2008 | |
| □ | ► E 0.64km | | ☺ | **Beaver Bonus Cache part 2** by Squeezy Sue | GC1C5F5 | United Kingdom | ⚲ | 1/2 | 05/11/2008 | 10/06/2013 10/23/2008 | |
| □ | ◄ W 0.68km | **1** | ☆ | **Cuerden Valley Park: Sleeping Beauty** by countrymatters | GC1Q5N5 | Northwest England, United Kingdom | ◉ | 3.5/2.5 | 04/17/2009 | Today* | |

this location' near the top of the list of caches your search has generated. A map will be displayed, showing the whereabouts of all the listed caches as small icons. When you find a cache the icon changes to a 'Smiley'.

This facility works for both basic and premium membership levels.

- **Column 1** is simply a selection column.
- **Column 2** gives the distance and direction of the cache from your home co-ordinates, with the nearest listed first.
- **Column 3** shows whether the cache in question has received any 'Favourite' points, awarded by other geocachers.
- **Column 4** is blank, but will have a 'Smiley' placed in it automatically once you've found the cache and recorded your find online. When you start placing caches of your own, this column will also contain a star icon to that effect.
- **Column 5** contains icons that tell you what type the cache is. Chapter 4 explains the different cache types, but to begin with choose a cache that looks like a green-topped brick; these are known as 'traditional' caches – the basic type.
- **Column 6** contains a range of information indicating caches that might need maintenance (red spanner);

List of geocaches from a given waypoint. The difference in colour distinguishes caches you own (pale yellow) and those you have to find or have found

'Under a rock', Isle of Skye

those that contain Travel bugs or geocoins; and those that are available only to Premium members.

- **Column 7** gives some information about the ease with which the cache might be found and retrieved. The letters 'D/T' indicate 'Difficulty' and 'Terrain' – in other words, how difficult the cache is to find, and how complex the terrain is that you will need to cross to get to it. The numbers 1/1 are the easiest, with 5/5 being (often) inordinately difficult. Also in this column, the little grey panel with a red square indicates the approximate size of the cache you're looking for, with the smallest square being on the left-hand side and the largest on the right.
- **Column 8** tells you the date on which the cache was placed.
- **Column 9** tells you when the cache was last found (and if you've found it, when you did so – green date in white rectangle). An asterisk indicates a cache that has been found in the last seven days.
- **Column 10** shows a small icon of a GPS device. This is a way in which you can download co-ordinate information from the website directly to your GPS device. This requires the free Garmin Communicator software – see above.

Countersunk concrete trig point – there are only a few of this type of trig point. This is on the summit of Branstree, and there is another on the summit of Blencathra (both in the Lake District)

The dramatic rock formations of Kilt Rock on the Isle of Skye are perfect examples of the kind of geological structures that underpin the earth science requirements of all EarthCaches

# 4 SELECTING GEOCACHES TO FIND

To begin with it's a good idea to select a cache close to your home – one you can walk to easily without causing concern to anyone in your family that you're going off into the wilderness in search of buried treasure and may never come back. Once you've found your first cache, suddenly everything starts to fall into place and make sense. There's also a certain excitement about your first find.

## DO YOUR HOMEWORK

Your search adventure begins at home as you query the database and compile your list of possible caches to find, as described in Chapter 3.

It's easiest to begin with a traditional cache (the ones with the green-topped brick icon), so for the moment ignore any of the others.

But before you dash out there are a few other issues to consider:
- Do you intend to go out alone, or with a friend or members of your family?
- Is everyone equally agile – could they cope with stiles and gates, for example?
- Will you be taking a dog with you?

Now check the attributes of the cache to see whether it's in a family-friendly location, or is open to dogs, open all hours, or involves a significant walk. The attributes enable you to find an easy cache to begin with – one that satisfies your requirements. There are a great many attributes, as you'll discover when you start placing caches yourself, but only eight can be displayed.

## GATHERING CACHE INFORMATION

When deciding on a geocache you want to look for, keep in mind the following:
- Have you considered the **difficulty and terrain ratings** of the cache? It makes sense to choose a 1/1 D/T rating for your first geocache find so that you can learn how geocaches are placed. However, 1/1 really is very easy, and (perhaps surprisingly) there may not be many – or any – near your home. For a first search you could realistically tackle anything up to a 2.5/2.5.

Once you've found a cache you want to search for, first check the logs entered by other geocachers. These appear at the bottom of the individual cache pages. From these logs you can obtain information that may help you in your search or, more importantly, tell you if the cache is missing. Each log entry gives the date on which the cache was found. If you encounter a run of entries indicating that the cache was not found, it may well have been lost or removed. In that case, find a different cache to start with.

These tree roots, which conceal a 2/2.5 cache, can prove slippery to the unwary

Remember: caches are concealed, not buried. You won't have to go armed with a spade to dig things up, but you may have to get into some muddy or awkward situations.

- Consult the **maps** of the area. Is this an urban or rural cache? And how might this change your planning? Road maps may be adequate in a town or city, but topographical maps, such as the Ordnance Survey Explorer or Landranger series, and the specialist maps produced by Harvey Maps – all of which show land and water features – may be more useful elsewhere. The OS Explorer and Harvey maps tell you which types of terrain you will encounter, while the former also give an indication of what's known as 'Access Land', where you may roam freely.

- Keep in mind that **distances** can be deceiving. Understand the difference between distances in a direct line and the actual distance of travel. You could be metres from a cache according to your GPS device, but there might be a river or other obstacle in the way. Part of the fun is that you have to find the best route to a cache, and usually it is not direct.

- Once you're close to the cache location you can **navigate** using your GPS device. For instance, if you're in a small park, you can try to simply follow the GPS arrow. In a large park this method might be challenging, so follow the established trails as much as possible while still keeping the GPS arrow heading in the general direction of the cache location. Don't go stomping through undergrowth, causing damage, only to find there was a path a short distance away!

Preparation and research will vary for each cache. Many geocachers begin with an online map to get an idea of the area, and then decide to supplement this with a detailed paper map.

## TYPES OF CACHE
There is a potentially bewildering range of caches, some with a number of variations on a theme, and some that have been discontinued.

### Traditional cache
This is the most common and most basic of caches – a simple container with a logbook in it. Typically these are Tupperware-like plastic boxes that can be locked, although containers that once held 35mm film are increasingly being used. Likewise, caches often take the form of old ammunition boxes or very small specimen bottles. For a traditional cache, the co-ordinates given on the cache page give its location (but see 'A question of accuracy', below).

### Multi-cache
A multi- (or multiple) cache may well take the physical form of a traditional cache, but it will involve three or more locations from which you obtain information – contained in the cache container or at the given location, for example a plaque on a wall – that leads to the final cache location. There are a number of variations in this group: some multi-caches simply form a trail to follow, with each cache containing a hint or co-ordinates that will guide you to another

If you plan to tackle a sequence of caches, mark these on a paper map so that you can more easily plan a route between them. But beware: while a mile of walking may take 20 minutes or so, a mile of geocaching can easily take double the time.

This 3/4.5 EarthCache is a long way out on desolate moorland. Are you properly equipped?

SELECTING GEOCACHES TO FIND

cache, and so on, until you reach the final cache; others contain letters or numbers, which, having been gained from successive caches, are used to calculate the co-ordinates of the final, bonus cache. (The most demanding of this type is arguably GC154N9: Little Quest, which involves visiting every county in England!) The most basic of these involves picking up one letter/number at each of ten traditional caches, with those numbers completing the co-ordinates of the final cache.

Other formats may take you to, say, only four caches, and then tell you that A+B=G, C-A=J, D÷B=F, and so on. The permutations are virtually endless. In this sort of format it is not unusual for the figures of degrees to be provided – for example N 54° and W 002° – because these will be fairly constant for your local area.

## Offset cache

Caches that require you to go to one location and get information – such as dates on a monument or a memorial plaque – from which to calculate the co-ordinates of the actual cache are known as 'offset caches'. Caches typical of this type provide information that enables you to complete, for example, the co-ordinates:

N    54°    AB.CDE
W    002°    FG.HIJ

## Mystery and puzzle caches

As the name suggests, these caches are for the dedicated puzzlers – those who love to wrestle with code-breaking, cryptic clues, cyphers, origami, and so on. It can take a long time to decipher some of the co-ordinate information, so you either have to rise to the challenge or stick to straight-forward, uncomplicated caches.

Typical puzzles might involve using a particular font from a conventional computer, such as:

Others may use a simple substitution code:

| A | B | C | D | E | F | G | H | I | J |
|---|---|---|---|---|---|---|---|---|---|
| 1 | 2 | 3 | 4 | 5 | 6 | 7 | 8 | 9 | 0 |

But the more complicated puzzle caches use a bewildering variety of cyphers and codes, including matrix or binary codes (GC1RM4W: The Matrix has you); the Pigpen cypher (also known as the Masonic cypher and used by Dan Brown in his book *The Lost Symbol* – such as GC1WYDR: Camel and Magna's Farmyard Cache); clock

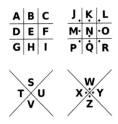

Other code examples:
Pigpen cypher (top) and The
Witching Hour clock faces
(bottom)

faces (GC40AVZ: 00:00~Midnight~The Witching Hour);
or just a long story from which you have to glean information (GC1NH60: Werewolf). Some use combinations of
two or more codes.

All of these puzzles are infuriatingly difficult and time-
consuming to crack, but they provide endless preoccupation
for those who like a challenge. To make matters worse, the
creativity and ingenuity of some geocachers is making this
type of cache both popular and increasingly complex. For
evidence of this, take a look at GCP5MD: The Clairvoyant,
and GCJRQ1: You sank my battleship. In short, you can
expect hours of puzzlement every time you encounter a
mystery cache with a difficulty rating of 4.5 or 5.

### Letterbox-hybrid cache

Letterboxing was a forerunner of geocaching. In its original
format you were given clues instead of co-ordinates in order
to locate a pot (the letterbox) containing a rubber stamp
and a visitors' book. More recently, letterbox hybrids have

evolved; these are a combination of conventional geocaching co-ordinates posted on the website, and a cache that contains a rubber stamp that you can use to record your visit. In practice this means that if you're searching for letterbox-hybrid caches you'll need to carry a small inkpad for use with the stamp. The stamp must remain in the cache but an inkpad would dry out quickly and become unusable, so they tend not to be left in caches.

### EarthCaches™

An EarthCache does not have a physical cache container. EarthCaches are special places you can visit to learn about a particular aspect of Earth science. EarthCache pages contain the usual co-ordinate information, but they also have extended notes on the significance of the cache location. EarthCaches are intended to convey an educational aspect that enables visitors to see how the Earth has been shaped by geological processes (see GC2D6AM: Elgol Honeycomb).

Visiting EarthCaches is an enjoyable experience for all the family, and participants are relieved of the responsibility of trying to find a concealed cache. You can identify EarthCaches near you by using the 'EarthCache listings' option on www.earthcache.org.

When you arrive at an EarthCache location you'll need to take certain action to confirm that you've been there. This will involve answering a series of questions relevant to the site (see 'Creating an EarthCache' in Chapter 7).

### Event caches

From time to time groups of geocachers will get together to organise a social event, ranging from an evening meal in a pub to an organised outing searching collectively for caches. These might coincide with dates such as the summer solstice, historical events, New Year's Day, and so on, and they are simply a medium for local and regional geocachers to get together and socialise. Because the event is a cache in itself, attendance gains you a point score in your overall tally of caches found. However, the cache is archived shortly after the event – so you have to be quick! Large gatherings of this type are known as 'mega-event caches', attended by at least 500 geocachers, but the principles are fundamentally the same.

### Cache In Trash Out (CITO) caches

Cache In Trash Out (CITO) is an ongoing environmental initiative supported by the worldwide geocaching community. Since 2002, geocachers have sought to clean up parks and other cache-friendly places around the world. All events are organised by volunteers and help preserve the natural beauty of our countryside.

Groundspeak celebrates annual international CITO events, where geocachers have an opportunity to participate in co-ordinated worldwide clean-up efforts. Geocachers host CITO events in their local area on the same day or weekend as other geocachers around the world. Together, these events make an enormous positive impact and generate a lot of fun for the participants in the process. With the permission of Cadw (the historic environment service of the Welsh government), the UK's first CITO event took place at Flint Castle, Flintshire, Wales, in July 2004, with a get-together featuring a buffet.

## Whereigo caches

Wherigo, the newest form of geocache, is a platform that allows you to build location-based GPS experiences on your computer and play them in the real world. Rather than using a computer mouse to select a location to move a character, as you would in a video game, with Whereigo caches you physically move from one location to the next to advance the story. So rather than searching for puzzle clues on a screen, you look for them in the real world. To search for Whereigo caches, however, you need to download the appropriate Whereigo cartridge to your smartphone. These are available from www.wherigo.com, and from the usual app download centres, such as Apple Store and Google Play.

## YOSM caches

Ye Ole Survey Monument caches are unique and are linked directly to just one cache (GC45CC). These are explained more fully in Chapter 10, but they are a type of travelling virtual cache.

## Grandfathered caches

The expression 'grandfathered' relates to cache types that are no longer available for creation, but which still exist to be found. Examples of these are as follows:

- **Virtual caches** – this type of cache exists only in the form of a location (there is no physical cache), but it is one that you have to visit. Once at the site of a virtual cache, you will have to answer a question about the location, or about someone who lived or worked nearby. The 'reward' for these caches is the actual location, and then sharing information about your visit. GCE387 is a classic example: the Palace of Westminster in London, otherwise known as the Houses of Parliament and Big Ben.

A webcam cache in the village of Coniston – notice the camera to the left of the left-hand chimney. These caches are no longer permitted as 'new' caches, but most of the old ones remain active

- **Webcam caches** – this interesting form of cache is difficult to complete because it involves someone else in addition to yourself. Across the country there are a number of places where webcams have been positioned. What you have to do is get yourself in front of the camera in order to record your visit; the difficult part is that you need someone to sit at a computer, logged on to www.geocaching.com and the cache page in particular, and capture the image. The webcam image on the cache page refreshes from time to time, so your task is to get someone to save the image with you in it, thus proving you were there. With the development of mobile broadband and WiFi internet connections, however, it is possible for you to use a hand-held device or small laptop to make the connections yourself as you stand in front of the camera. It's all a little high-tech, but good fun.

- **Cuckoo caches** – this type of cache is a travelling cache, a cache within a cache; find one and you find two. Your task is then to take the cuckoo cache to a different cache and leave it there for someone else to find and move on, although this is not obligatory (you can leave it where it is). In many ways it's like a conventional trackable item (see Chapter 8). GC4C35 is a typical example of a cuckoo cache.

### Handicaching
The website www.handicaching.com allows cache owners to rate their caches with the aim of improving the accessibility of geocaching for disabled people. Using this system you can rate caches that you own, as well as caches that you've found.

## THE SIZE OF CACHES
The bigger the cache container, the easier it is (theoretically) to find. For some time, before they became militaria collectors' items, old ammunition boxes were used, and while these can still be found, there are few new caches appearing that use this type of container.

Increasingly, geocachers are using lockable plastic containers that are available from supermarkets, although it is possible to buy geocaching-specific boxes from a number of online sources. See also Chapter 7.

Near the top of the cache page you'll find information about the size of the cache you're looking for, and this should be noted.

## A QUESTION OF ACCURACY
You might think that if you're armed with cache co-ordinates you can walk straight up to a cache location – and sometimes this is the case. But more often you'll find that the co-ordinates appear to be slightly inaccurate. The reasons for this are partly to do with inconsistencies in information transmitted by satellites (see Chapter 2), but more often the inaccuracies are related to factors that can restrict 'satellite view' and so give less than spot-on readings, such as trees, overhanging cliffs and tall buildings. The cache owner will have tried to get the best possible reading, but it may not correspond exactly with the location of the cache. More to the point, there is a skill in recording co-ordinate information (see Chapter 7), and if the original cache owner

Sleeping Beauty

**Section taken from Google Earth**

does not have that skill, the co-ordinates themselves may be inaccurate. See 'Adding revised co-ordinates' in Chapter 6 to learn what to do about this.

## GOOGLE EARTH

The basic version of Google Earth is downloadable free from www.google.com and provides high-resolution satellite images of the Earth. With a bit of practice you can zoom in on the locality of your cache search, get some idea of the terrain, and even place a marker at the exact co-ordinates of the cache. The detail is outstanding, and is particularly useful in identifying convenient places to park a car.

The Google Earth image is also useful in planning your approach to a cache location and weighing up the obstacles you might encounter. Of course, tree cover conceals everything, but as a guide Google Earth has much to commend it.

Google Earth supports what are known as KML files – specially formatted files, created for Google Earth, containing data that is viewed only when using Google Earth on a desktop computer. The KML data derived from www.geocaching.com includes information such as geocache name, type and D/T ratings, which are all easily browsed in the Google Earth mapping interface. However, the co-ordinates used in Google Earth are only approximate, and could be out by 30+m (100ft).

### How to view geocaches using Google Earth

- Download the Geocaching Google Earth Viewer from 'Your Profile' (right-hand column). This produces a KML file. Click on the file and Google Earth will open.
- Input a location in the text box at the top-left of the Google Earth side menu.
- Geocaches within the map view will then be shown as geocache icons. Click on an icon to view specific geocache information, including cache size and difficulty/terrain ratings.
- Click on the GC code to view the cache detail page on www.geocaching.com.

**Don't overlook the obvious when searching for a cache**

Checking your location using map and compass is a useful skill in geocaching

# 5 SEARCHING FOR A GEOCACHE

At a basic level, searching for a geocache involves no more than storing the cache co-ordinates in a GPS device, and then going out to find it using the GPS alone. But it is rarely as simple as that.

Even so, this is where the fun begins, and the satisfaction of finding caches never abates. Find 10 and you'll want to make it 20, then 50 and 100, 200, 300, 1000. With over two million caches worldwide, you won't run out.

On 28 February 2013 it was announced that there were, as at that time, two million active geocaches worldwide

## WHAT TO TAKE WITH YOU
In deciding what to take with you, much will depend on how many caches you are hoping to find, what distance lies between them, and how long you plan to be out. If you're making a day of it, a map, compass, GPS and suitable clothing and footwear are all obvious items to take. In this respect, geocaching is no different to going out for a walk (although it will be more time-consuming) and you should be appropriately equipped – you may spend a good deal of time relatively inactive and getting cold. It's useful, too, to print out the cache information from the website and carry it with you.

You'll also need a pen to sign logbooks. Many caches already contain pens and/or pencils, but this cannot be guaranteed, so get into the habit of taking your own – preferably one that's waterproof (logbook pages are often damp).

Other items that have been found useful include:
- a pair of tweezers (for extracting rolled-up logs from small cache containers)
- a magnet
- a pocket knife (to help open some of the more difficult containers, and to sharpen pencils)

- a torch and spare batteries (to check the insides of pipes, for example, or to search in poorly lit locations such as among tree roots, in tunnels or down holes)
- a pair of gloves (to protect hands when searching for caches concealed in prickly or stinging locations, and to search in holes that might be occupied – we do have adders in the UK, and they do not like to be disturbed)
- a walking stick or pole (with which to poke about in holes or bushes).

It's also good practice – and courteous – to carry a few small plastic bags which can be used to protect caches that may have become wet or damaged, and even a small notebook in case you find the existing logbook full. If either of these scenarios are encountered, you have the option, when logging your find on www.geocaching.com, to leave a 'maintenance' note for the owner, explaining what's necessary and what you've done as an interim measure.

You may also have 'travellers' – Travel bugs and geocoins (see Chapter 8) – that you want to take, or items that you want to leave in the cache. Occasionally you may be asked to take a photograph of yourself or a location to prove that you were there, so that means taking a camera, too – although the images produced by many mobile phones are perfectly adequate for geocaching purposes.

**Ladybird cache: someone has created a small cache and disguised it by using a ladybird toy. Caches like this are always favourites with children**

## SEARCH STRATEGIES

Once you move beyond searching for single caches to searching for a series, it makes sense to have a basic strategy and technique. Everyone does this in a different way, and you may well devise your own. But here is a basic strategy to use as a starting point – which you will no doubt refine (or discard) as you become more experienced:

- Begin by **plotting the cache locations on a map**. If you look at the cache page you'll see that beneath the co-ordinates in latitude and longitude the location is given in terms of the British Grid system. This allows you to roughly pinpoint the location on a map. You can also check with www.streetmap.co.uk to be sure you have the location approximately correct.

- Now **study the map** and figure out how you can legally link all the caches together in one circular walk (assuming you want to get back to your starting point). In this context, and if the caches are in the countryside, Ordnance Survey maps at 1:25,000 scale show Access Land – areas of land, usually upland or moorland, where you can wander freely without having to stay on public rights of way. However, it's worth remembering that footpaths evolved where they did for a reason, and that reason may well be the difficulty of the ground to either side of it. Wandering freely isn't always a good idea.

- **Download the co-ordinates** to your GPS device and check they're there. Note, however, that your GPS will show only those caches that are close to the current GPS location – for example, your home. If you're in the UK and you download co-ordinates for caches in, say, France, they will not be displayed on the GPS until the device has actually located your position in France. But beware! Remember to delete your French caches before you return home, as once you're back in the UK they will remain on your device but won't be displayed, thus taking up GPS memory (see Chapter 9 for information on how to download cache information in bulk).

- If you haven't printed out the cache information, then at least **carry a small notebook**, and in it enter the cache code (GC followed by four or more digits or letters), its name (because often there is a clue in the name) and, if you want to do this, decrypt the clue and write that information in your notebook too – or at least enter the encrypted string of characters with a view to decrypting them later, out in the field, should you have difficulty finding the cache.

- Check that you have **spare batteries** for your GPS, or a solar charger.

The spectacular geology along the ascent of Ingleborough
from Crina Bottom is ideal for the creation of an EarthCache

- When you get to your starting point, **check** with the map **that you're following the correct route**. You can enter key landmark features – such as bridges and road junctions – into your GPS as waypoints, and use these to navigate along the route. But remember that if you use only cache co-ordinates, the GPS device will show only straight-line connections, and it may not be possible to walk in a straight line.

## GETTING CLOSE

Your GPS device will get you fairly close to the cache location, but bear in mind that accuracy is a rather vague notion, affected not least by the disposition of satellites and the skill of the cache owner in taking the original readings when the cache was put in place. Some GPS devices will emit an audible signal as you approach the cache co-ordinates ('ground zero' or 'GZ'), but it's rare that the co-ordinates and the actual location coincide precisely. Now is the moment to put your own skills to the test:

- Begin by thinking about the **cache container**. The cache page tells you whether this is large or small, and some may give even more information – such as whether it's an ammunition box, film container, cigar case, or one of the newer, very small containers such as bisons and nanos. So, for example, an ammunition box is not going to be concealed in a narrow fissure in a rock.
- Many **cache containers are camouflaged**, so what you're looking for is a shape that doesn't belong in a natural landscape. The more geocaching you do, the more you'll learn to recognise what's natural and what isn't – straight lines and perfect circles rarely occur in nature.
- Once you arrive at the cache co-ordinates take a moment to **scan the terrain**, rather than moving haphazardly across it. Look at the lie of the land and try to figure out what would make a good hiding place. Bearing in mind that caches are concealed, not buried, popular hiding places include cracks in rocks, the bases of trees, tree stumps, fallen logs, natural hollows and piles of rocks. 'Microcaches' are a particularly stern challenge to anyone's observational skills and patience: by their nature these are small objects in a large space, and spotting them is not easy, but it is rewarding when you achieve it.
- While searching for a cache you need to be constantly on the lookout for **anything that looks unnatural**: 'organised' piles of twigs and branches ('stickoflage', for want of a better expression); groups of stones that look

just a little too tidy; or piles of rocks that have a different colouration from the surrounding rocks. As time goes by you'll learn to spot these differences from a distance.

- When you reach the cache location, **ask yourself where you would conceal a cache** and look there first. Trusting intuition is something all geocachers do. Begin by checking the obvious hiding places.

- If a thorough search of GZ doesn't reveal the cache, **widen your search area**, bearing in mind the in-built inaccuracies in location as mentioned above. Quite often just a few strides away will make all the difference.

## THE TROUBLE WITH 'MUGGLES'

As any fan of *Harry Potter* will understand, a 'muggle' (in geocaching terms) is someone who doesn't geocache. Inevitably, when out geocaching, you will encounter muggles. The trouble with muggles is that they don't know what geocaching is about, so it's vital to ensure the security of caches by searching for, locating, retrieving and replacing cache containers when there are no muggles about. This can be challenging in itself – especially with caches concealed in town centre parks, along main roads, on housing estates or in shopping centres, for example.

Gnomes from home – someone has created a small cache shelter for these guardian gnomes

Stealth is all-important, and you may have to suspend searching if muggles approach, resuming again once they've passed. Trying to look nonchalant often works, but it's only a small step from looking suspicious; the last thing you want is the sudden appearance of authority enquiring what you're up to. If you are approached, say, by a policeman, be polite and explain geocaching. Following a bomb scare in Wetherby in 2012 the police authorities have been made aware of geocaching, so while not every constable will know about it, the greater policing community does.

There are many ways of diverting attention when muggles approach. It's amazing how many geocachers suddenly find the need to re-tie shoelaces, pick up something that appears to have fallen from a pocket, or seem to be making a call on a mobile phone that only close inspection shows to be a GPS device. A loud-ish and animated 'phone' conversation is certain to keep passing muggles at bay. Carrying a camera and pretending to take shots of leaves, flowers, lichen or rock formations is another technique. Just remember to be casual: if you behave suspiciously, people will

**Geocaches are to be found throughout the UK, including in the countryside, where geocaching offers a great alternative to crowded beaches (photo: Mark Fishwick)**

see you as suspicious – but everyone's entitled to stare at drainpipes!

The point of all this subterfuge is to make certain that inquisitive muggles do not attempt to see what you've been up to after you leave. Each year, caches disappear because they've been 'muggled'; muggling ranges from malicious to unintentional, but every loss is a loss to the pursuit until the cache is replaced.

## MAP AND COMPASS TECHNIQUES

The ability to use a map and compass, while not critical, does help in the search for geocaches. At the very least, being able to understand and read a topographic map (such as an Ordnance Survey map) does enable you to get an approximate fix on the location of a cache and to assess what obstacles might lie in the way. Using a map such as this enables you to plan a route to link caches, and to navigate around unexpected obstacles such as rivers, buildings, steep ground and woodland.

For a detailed exposition of map and compass techniques, you might usefully consult *Map and Compass: The Art of Navigation* by Pete Hawkins (Cicerone Press, 2013), or the author's own *Map Reading Skills* (Crimson Publishing, 2007). Both explain at some length how to acquire and develop the skills of navigation.

## SOME COURTESY AND SAFETY CONSIDERATIONS

Although geocaching should be no more hazardous a pastime than recreational walking, there are a few additional considerations:

Geocaching can take you into close proximity with barbed wire fences, rusty gates and the like, as well as into places where you might be nettled or scratched. Readers may wish to consider a tetanus injection, as a safeguard.

- **Be aware of your responsibilities** as a walker and observe the Countryside Code (www.naturalengland.org.uk).
- **Consider taking someone with you**, especially if you're going into remote or difficult terrain.
- **Leave a note** in a conspicuous place in your car to say where you're going, possibly giving the cache co-ordinates; that way, if you become lost people will know where to look for you. It's a debateable issue as to whether you give an indication of the expected time of return, as this simply tells thieves how long they have to break into your car. In any case, you'll take much longer than you think!
- **Put the co-ordinates for your car into your GPS** as a waymark; it's easy to become disorientated, especially in woodland areas.
- **Take plenty to eat and drink**.

The author finds a cache deep within a cave on the Isle of Skye

- Before you go, **check the weather forecast**, and, while out on the search, keep an eye on the sky and pay attention to the passage of time.
- During the grouse-shooting season or periods of deer stalking, **check with the relevant estates** that it's safe for you to go, and, if necessary, be prepared to change your plans.
- **Do not touch discarded items** – they could be hazardous.
- Do not forget to **look up from your GPS from time to time** to avoid walking over cliff edges or into ditches, and to spot potholes, overhanging branches or other obstructions.
- Should you get into difficulties and have to phone for help, remember that your GPS will give your precise location. The smartphone app 'OS Locate' will do the same, using the British Grid.

A splendid EarthCache: the Giant's Causeway, Northern Ireland

# 6  DISCOVERING A GEOCACHE

The primary aim of geocaching is to find concealed caches, and to have fun while you're doing it. Simple enough, you might think. But what do you have to do when you actually discover a cache? Is there an 'etiquette' to be observed? And what do you do if you've been unable to find a cache?

## WHAT TO DO WHEN YOU FIND A GEOCACHE

Caches will seldom be in plain view. You may hit on one almost immediately, or you may spend some considerable time hunting around, trying to look nonchalant so as not to draw attention to yourself. Even the best geocachers fail sometimes to notice what's in front of them; it's amazing what you don't see when you don't know what you're looking for!

Once you have the cache container in your hands, enjoy the moment and the sense of accomplishment that goes with it – this is, after all, something you located and retrieved by your own endeavour. You can feel chuffed – no-one's watching!

One of the first things to do is to take a moment to note how, and precisely where, the container was concealed, bearing in mind that when you eventually leave the site you'll need to replace the cache exactly as it was found. Another key point at this early stage is to take a quick look around to ensure you're not being observed.

Now walk away from the site with the container in your hand. If it's convenient to do so, perch on a rock or a bench and look as though you're taking a breather or having a bite to eat. Cache containers that really are Tupperware 'lunch' boxes are excellent for this little subterfuge.

## OPENING THE CACHE

Depending on the age of the cache, it may be in pristine condition or it may be grubby and damaged. If it's damaged there's a good chance water has penetrated the container, leaving whatever's inside it in a mess. So take care opening the container, just in case. If it's filled with water and everything in it is sodden, then, if you're equipped to do so, attempt some kind of repair (although some caches will be beyond redemption). Tip out the water and do your best to make the container dry. Remove any sodden items from the

If you're searching with children and you're the first to find the cache, consider pretending that you didn't, and then directing one of the children to the spot so that they discover it. They'll enjoy the experience all the more, and will be more willing to try geocaching again.

**Official log book**

container and take them away for disposal, but leave the log in place, however wet it is – you can send a maintenance message to the cache owner when you log your visit on the website.

Because cache containers come in all shapes and sizes, the opening 'mechanism' will vary; some are simple plastic clip locks, others have flip tops, while many of the smaller ones screw together. In recent years, old plastic medicine bottles have started to appear – the kind that have infuriating 'child-proof' tops that only a child can open! Some cache containers are fitted with locks, the opening of which invariably requires ingenuity and the resolution of a number of tests.

## SIGNING THE LOG

Each cache contains a record log of some kind. Those that are large enough hold small notebooks, some purpose-made and others improvised. You may also find pencils (for signing the log – don't remove them) and even pencil sharpeners.

The very small cache containers (nanos and bisons) hold a rolled-up or folded strip of paper in place of a notebook. These serve just as well, but can be notoriously difficult to extricate from the cache container, and equally difficult to put back.

The logbook is a record of everyone who has found the cache. It's interesting to spend a few minutes looking through the log entries and reading what fun others may have had finding the cache. The more you 'cache' around your local area, the more names you'll come to recognise. Many of these geocachers you may subsequently meet at a local event cache.

Go to the next available space in the logbook and make your own entry (the chronology of this is not critical: the author often chooses to sign in space left by other finders in order to prolong the life of the log book as much as possible). An absolute minimum is your geocaching name and the date; if you happen to be the first to find the cache (FTF), then you should enter the time, too. It's an agreeable and considerate part of the pursuit to add a few comments, including the names of any other geocachers with you, and to say something about your search for the cache – the weather, the terrain conditions and so on. At the very least it's courtesy to enter 'TFTC' (Thanks for the cache) and 'TNLN' (Took nothing, left nothing, if appropriate) – but see 'Trading', below, and 'Trackable items' in Chapter 8.

Some geocachers have rubber stamps with which to stamp the logbook, or custom-made adhesive labels to fix into the log.

Some cache containers are so small, however, that all you can do is enter the date and your initials. You should not use up space in a small logbook by entering extended messages. Keep it simple.

A few caches contain small cameras that visitors are asked to use to take a picture of themselves at the cache site. The cache owner makes periodic visits to retrieve the camera, and then posts the pictures on the geocaching website. If you encounter such a cache you need to be clear that the camera is not a trading item (see below), and should be left in the cache.

The rocks in the foreground of this picture are a perfect site for concealing a cache, but it may still take a while before you actually locate it

A fundamental rule of geocaching is that you sign the log as proof that you found it. However, there are many instances when you cannot sign the log: perhaps it's too wet to sign or has disintegrated; perhaps it cannot physically be extracted from the container (often the case with smaller caches) or the container would not open. If this is the case, log your find on the cache page as normal, but then email the cache owner to let them know about the problem with the log. You can most usefully do this via a 'Needs maintenance' log. Quite often, in this type of situation, it's useful to take a photograph of the container to show that you did actually retrieve it.

DISCOVERING A GEOCACHE

However, if your reason for not signing the log is because you can't reach it – because it's up a tree, for example – then you should not claim the find. Each cache is given a Difficulty and Terrain rating, with which you are credited once you log your find; if you do not succeed in retrieving the cache, even if you could see it, then you do not earn the D/T rating.

## TRADING

One of the underlying principles of geocaching is 'trading' – that is, putting some trinket or 'treasure' into a cache and taking something out. Of course, this is possible only with containers large enough to take items, but the basic rule is that you should 'trade up' – in other words, put in something of greater worth than you take out.

In reality, the business of trading up is not always feasible, because each time there is a trade the items put in the cache are (in theory) of higher value, and there's a limit to how far you go – it would take some trading up to replace the wrist watch (still ticking away after four winter months) found in one Lake District cache, or the functioning digital device for measuring map distances found in southern Scotland.

In practice, trading up has evolved into 'swapping' – in other words, put something in and take something out, regardless of value. This particular aspect of geocaching is of special appeal to children, who may well find small toys and games in caches. One cache in Lancashire is used by www.bookcrossing.com as a repository for books: leave behind a book you've read and take another in its place. You need to be registered as a member of BookCrossing, and you do still need to find the cache containing the books, but it adds another appealing dimension to the pursuit.

If you don't have anything to trade, the correct thing to do is simply to sign the logbook and take nothing (TNLN). Don't take something without leaving anything in its place. The exceptions to this rule are Travel bugs and geocoins (see Chapter 8).

As you discover more caches, so you get a better idea of the sort of things people leave behind. Rarely, if ever, is it anything unsavoury – and nor should it be. It can be just about anything that'll fit into the cache container, but here are some guidelines:

- **Do not leave food items**, not even sweets – food attracts animals, and some containers have been chewed into

or knocked about by foxes and badgers looking for something to eat.

- **Do not leave anything that is illegal, dangerous or potentially offensive** – geocaching is a family activity; be considerate and responsible.
- If you're trading, **try to leave something of at least equal value** – don't, for example, take a small piece of jewellery and leave a plastic toy from a burger bar.
- **Clear out the rubbish** – some caches gradually fill up with trash, broken toys, cheap plastic stuff, battered golf balls, rusting badges and so on, and these should be removed. But also, over time, some items deteriorate in quality. So, as a guide, if the items in the cache are not something you would happily put in your coat pocket, put them in a carrier bag and ditch them in a rubbish bin at the first opportunity. It does no harm and a lot of good to maintain caches in this way, even if they're not your own. This is called 'community maintenance'; there's nothing more disappointing than a cache that is not maintained.
- **Think about what you put in** – is the next visitor likely to find your trade item interesting, useful or fun?

## RETURNING THE CACHE CONTAINER

Before you leave the cache location, you must return the container to its original place and conceal it properly. Here are a few tips you might follow in doing so:

- Make a point of checking to **ensure that the container is properly closed** – there's nothing worse than opening a cache container that's full of stagnant water because the previous finder didn't close it properly.
- **Put the cache back where you found it**, concealed at least as well as it was. Because caches occasionally get disturbed and are found in the open, or slightly exposed, it makes sense, and is good practice, to ensure that the cache is properly hidden. Don't make it more difficult to find, but do make it secure. And remember, one of the give-aways of a cache hiding place is that whatever is covering it does not look natural. Bear this in mind when replacing a cache.
- **Make sure you've left nothing behind** – and that includes lunch wrappers or tissues, as well as your GPS, mobile phone, car keys, camera, dog... and children.
- **Cover your tracks** – many caches can be found because previous finders have created a 'cachers' path' to them. Do your best to avoid this; try not to leave any evidence of your visit.

If you have a number of caches to log entries for, there's a little trick to speed up the process. It starts when you identify the caches you're going in search of. Go to the Navigation panel on the cache page and select 'Watch'. This will add the cache(s) to a page known as your 'Watchlist', which is accessible from your profile page. When you return home, simply go to your Watchlist and select the caches you've found; it's much quicker this way, even though this may not have been the original intention of the Watchlist. You should do this with all the caches you're going out to find; it just makes keeping a record a little easier. Once you've logged your find, remember to remove the cache from your Watchlist. The latest version of the geocaching website lists, under 'Quick view', the last five caches you looked at.

**6**

DISCOVERING A GEOCACHE

Gordale Scar in the Yorkshire Dales National Park poses a problem for walkers wanting to go up, but for geocachers is an easy EarthCache

## LOGGING YOUR FIND

Part of the fun of geocaching is in sharing your experience of finding a cache with others. You do this on the www. geocaching.com website by finding the cache you've located using any of the methods previously described, although the speediest is simply to enter the GC code on the home page of the website. You can log your find at any time – days, weeks or months after you found it – but it's a good idea to get into the habit of logging the find as soon as you can, so that you don't forget it.

To log a find, go to the Navigation panel on the cache page and select 'Log your visit'. You are then redirected to a page headed 'Post a new log', on which there are three main fields.

The first is the **'Type of log'** field – the main choices being 'Found it', 'Didn't find it', 'Write a note', 'Needs archiving' and 'Needs maintenance'. So, select 'Found it'.

Other entries in the 'Type of log' field are as follows:

- 'Didn't find it' – you looked for the cache but failed to find it (see 'What to do when you can't find a cache', below).
- 'Write a note' – notes are not logged as 'finds', but are used when you have something to say, for example that the cache logbook is full and needs replacing, or that you passed by the cache (having previously discovered it) and want to record that everything is okay with it.
- 'Needs archived' – choose this option if you found a serious problem with the cache (if it is badly damaged, for example). An archived cache is not active, but it remains in the database so that its information page can be viewed in order to discover why it was archived.
- 'Needs maintenance' – means just that: the cache is damaged, wet, or irreparable and needs the attention of the owner. When you select this option the owner is sent an email message about the problems with their cache.
- 'Attended' – this is the entry you make if you attend an event cache; this 'Type of log' option appears on the screen only for event caches. Before an event, you also have the option to select 'Will attend'.
- 'Webcam photo taken' – this is the correct log type for webcam caches, which, although 'discontinued', still have a number of active locations around the country. This log-type option appears only for webcam caches.

The second field on the 'Post a new log' page is the **date**, which defaults to the current date, but if this does not correspond with the date on which you actually made the find you can simply change it.

The third field is where you enter any **comments** you want to make about your experience: whether you enjoyed it, had terrain difficulties, fell in a river, met other geocachers, had to avoid muggles, cows, bulls... whatever you want to say. But it's important to say something – part of the fun of placing caches is the pleasure derived from others finding them and saying something nice about your efforts. So you should do the same in return. There's nothing worse than a string of logs that read 'TFTC' and nothing more; it just doesn't show any kind of appreciation for the efforts of the cache owner. Equally dubious are comments like 'Found on my holidays in Scotland' – if the cache is concealed in Scotland it can't be found anywhere else, so this kind of log is meaningless.

Sometimes, in your comment, you may want to make reference to something that'll give a clue to the cache location. To avoid this appearing too readily to those who have not yet found the cache, you have the option to encrypt the whole or part of your comment by selecting the 'Encrypt this log entry' key below the comments panel. For example, comments such as, 'We had to use a long stick to unhook the cache from the tree branch' are something of a giveaway that you might want to encrypt. If you do decide to encrypt a comment you should note that text within square brackets – [What a great cache!] – will not be encrypted. So you can put all your 'open' comments in square brackets and leave sections of your comments without brackets so that they become encrypted. There are no hard and fast rules about this; it's your decision.

When you've completed your log, simply click on 'Submit log entry'.

In completing a log, you also have the option to award a Favourite point. The number of **Favourite points** awarded to caches is displayed at the top of the cache page. The system automatically gives you 100 starter Favourite points that you can award to caches that have particularly pleased you, and you earn more Favourite points the more caches you find. It's a nice gesture to award a Favourite point, to recognise the time and effort given by the cache owner.

## UPLOADING PICTURES

You might also want to upload a picture or two taken at the cache location – but be careful not to give too much away. Be wary of conspicuous features in the background, for example. However, geocaching is family fun and it's great for children to have their pictures on the website, showing them holding the cache container.

Uploading pictures from your computer is not difficult. Once you've logged your find, locate your log entry on the

**Found it!**

cache page (it'll be the first in the list at the bottom of the page) and click on 'Upload image', just below your log entry, to go through to 'Uploading for a Geocaching Log Image'. Choose the image from those on your computer, write a caption and click on 'Upload'.

The system supports the normal picture formats – JPEG, GIF and TIF – although all the final images are converted to JPEG format.

## ADDING REVISED CO-ORDINATES

There may be times when you find a cache and discover that the co-ordinates on your GPS receiver do not correspond with those on the cache page. Slight differences, up to 10 metres, are tolerable and to be expected, but if there's a significant difference, and you can be certain that you were receiving a strong satellite signal, you can post your co-ordinates on the website by ticking the box marked 'Add a co-ordinate to this log' on the 'Post a new log' page. This opens a panel in which you can insert your co-ordinates. Of course, you should then post a 'Comment' to explain why you found the co-ordinates to be different, but it's ultimately for the cache owner to change the co-ordinates, based on the information you give.

## WHAT TO DO WHEN YOU CAN'T FIND A CACHE

There are only two reasons why caches are not found: the first is that they are no longer there (muggled or moved by animals) and the second is your level of diligence. The latter is something that improves the more you geocache; the greater your experience, the more readily you can spot likely cache locations that you might previously have over-looked. It's no shame not to find a cache – finding them takes practice. Don't be put off. Speak to any experienced geocacher and they'll tell you many stories of caches they were unable to find, even of taking three or four attempts to find a cache that everyone else seemed to easily locate.

But the components of diligence in this context are many:

- How much time were you able to devote to your search?
- Are you sure you had the correct co-ordinates?
- Was there adequate satellite coverage to give you a strong signal?
- Did you check the log entries to see if others had also failed to find the cache?
- Did you check the hint?
- Were there too many muggles about?
- Was it getting dark?
- Were you systematic in your search?
- Were you distracted at a critical moment?

Whether it was because the cache was lost or you simply couldn't spot it, it's good practice to log DNF. This alerts the owner to the possibility that the cache may have gone missing and may need replacing. The owner won't respond to a solitary DNF, but if a series appears then it's a safe bet that something is awry.

It's equally important to return to a cache you couldn't find first time round in order to search again. Add it to your Watchlist to see if anyone else finds it. Geocaching is a fun activity; don't take it too seriously. When you do find the cache you'll be wondering how you missed it the first time. It happens to everyone!

If you fail to find (DNF), add the cache to your Watchlist. If anyone else finds, or does not find, the cache, you'll receive a note to that effect. If there's a string of DNFs you can feel moderately satisfied; it wasn't your fault. But if others come along and find the cache with ease, then you know what to do. Do not log a DNF if you didn't really look for the cache – perhaps because it was raining or there were too many muggles about. Log a DNF only if you genuinely searched (for more than a few minutes) but didn't find the cache. DNRB (Did not really bother) and DNT (Did not try) don't count.

## CACHES THAT HAVE NOT BEEN MAINTAINED

During your geocaching expeditions you may encounter caches that have not been maintained. This could be for a variety of reasons. The first step in the procedure for getting the cache serviced is to post a 'Needs maintenance' note on the website; this alerts the owner to the fact that something needs to be done about the cache. You do this as one of the options under 'Log your find'.

However, the owner may no longer be involved in geocaching, which effectively leaves the cache high and dry, or (more to the point) low and very wet. There's no provision for you to simply take over ownership of the cache; it belongs to someone else (although if some kind fairy were to visit the cache and replace the container with a new one, who would know?). You can, however, contact the owner and offer to take over the ownership. If they don't respond, all you can do is contact one of the reviewers and ask for the cache to be archived; the reviewer will follow a procedure that ultimately leads to the cache being archived. This then allows you to go out and create a new cache at that location.

A micro cache concealed in the hollowed-out base of a small log

DISCOVERING A GEOCACHE

The stunning landscape around Elgol on the Isle of Skye makes this a perfect candidate for an EarthCache

# 7 CREATING GEOCACHES

Sooner or later you'll want to try creating caches yourself, and this is every bit as enjoyable and challenging as searching for them. But it's something that requires a little forethought if you're to earn a reputation for quality caches. It's like writing a book – you begin with an idea, spend time planning and giving the idea shape, then give form to the idea, and finally sit back and see what people have to say about your handiwork.

Adding your own caches to the ever-increasing number throughout the world involves:

- deciding on the type of geocache to create
- selecting a container
- selecting a good hiding place
- determining the co-ordinates
- deciding on the cache contents
- submitting the cache for review (getting your cache published)
- maintaining the geocache.

Full guidelines on creating geocaches are contained on www.geocaching.com – begin by looking in 'Hide and seek a cache'. They're quite extensive and give a lot of detail, and the key points are summarised in the following paragraphs. When creating a cache you're required to indicate that you've read and understood these guidelines. Because all caches are located on someone's land, a team of reviewers will look at the details of your proposed cache to check whether it can be published on the website (see 'Submitting a geocache for review', below).

## DECIDING ON THE TYPE OF GEOCACHE TO CREATE

The easiest type of cache to begin with is a **traditional cache**, the basic format. As a minimum your traditional cache must contain some form of logbook.

One of the reasons for choosing a simple, straightforward cache type to begin with is that placing caches comes with an obligation to maintain them – in other words, checking them periodically, responding to logs telling you that the logbook is full/wet/missing, and so on. By keeping things simple to start with, you learn just how much is involved in placing caches. If you're happy with the responsibility, go

It makes sense not to attempt to place caches yourself until you've spent some time discovering how other geocachers do it. Searching for caches teaches you what to take into consideration when deciding on your own cache locations, and gives you ideas for hiding your own. Another consideration is that a high proportion of new geocachers fail to continue beyond their first year. If, during that year, they've created geocaches (and later lost interest in geocaching), the cache may not be retrieved, and will simply become geo-litter – which no-one wants.

ahead and place more. But – and this is a plea on behalf of all geocachers – if you feel you might be unable to maintain a cache, please do not place it. Caches on top of mountains are fine… until you have to maintain them.

Whether you move on to creating **multi-caches** or **puzzle caches** is something you can decide once you have a clear understanding of the skills that are involved in creating these caches. It's hugely rewarding to create a puzzle cache, for example, but you have to be certain that the solution to the puzzle really does give the correct information – and only the correct information. For example, the binary code:

01001110 00100000 00110101 00110011 11000010 10110000 00100000 00110100
00110010 00101110 00110110 00110110 00110000 00001101 00001010 01010111
00100000 00110000 00110000 00110010 11000010 10110000 00100000 00110011
00111000 00101110 00111001 00110001 00110100 00001101 00001010

translates as:
N   53°   42.660
W   002°   38.914

Even the slightest error while inputting this sort of eye-boggling information can result in wide deviations. So, to be certain that your encoding is done correctly you need a code translator, and there are a number of these on the internet. It's advisable to encode and decode the information a couple of times to be sure it is correct (see 'Geocaching co-ordinates checker' in Chapter 10).

### SELECTING A CONTAINER

The simplest form of container to use is a plastic food container with four lock-down clips, available from most supermarkets. The container should be waterproof, for obvious reasons, as you'll discover when you find some that were not.

A magnetic nano

A Pelican container

There may be many other suitable containers about your house, but for ease of getting started, spend a little to buy some of the Tupperware-like boxes and a supply of small notebooks to serve as logbooks. You might want to be indulgent and buy pencils and pencil sharpeners to place in the container; if not, you need to alert other geocachers to the fact that they'll have to bring a pen to sign the log. You do that in the cache description.

The beauty of the food-container type of box is that it allows for the placement of trade items and trackable items (see Chapter 8). This makes the cache more attractive to seekers. This type of container will serve equally well for the type of caches that are a little more challenging, such as multi-caches, puzzle caches and letterbox hybrids.

Other domestic containers that you can use include plastic medicine bottles, 35mm film canisters, and anything else that can be locked. Large boxes are generally easy to find, but at the other extreme there are cache containers known as nanos, which are very small (no more than a centimetre in diameter). They are also magnetic and can simply be fixed to any metal surface, thus blending in well with the background.

There's no particular need to invest in purpose-made cache containers, but they do have printed on them a notice that they're an 'Official geocache' and part of a worldwide game, and it enhances the image of the game if containers are properly labelled. You can buy labels from a number of sources, including the Geocaching Association of Britain (see page 131). More companies are now producing bespoke cache containers, many of them already camouflaged.

To make the pursuit even more interesting, it's possible to buy cache containers that are disguised as rocks, bolts, capsules, acorns, mushrooms, pine cones and a whole imaginative range of items. The aim is to make geocaching challenging, to encourage observation and search skills... and to develop persistence!

To prolong the life of your caches, use only containers that are watertight. Film canisters are fine in dry summer conditions, but they are not watertight. Ideal as they may be in terms of size, they do deteriorate very quickly. If you do use a film canister, wrap the log sheet in a plastic wallet to help keep it dry.

Use black or camouflage tape or paint to cover the plastic container and make it more difficult to detect. You can also buy or make camouflage bags in which to conceal containers.

## SELECTING A GOOD LOCATION AND HIDING PLACE

By now you will have found a few caches yourself, and will be getting an idea of the sort of locations that are suitable for hiding a cache. On your travels you may well have already noticed a few likely places.

If you create a cache more than 50 miles from your home, it's likely that the reviewer will want you to nominate a local maintainer. You have a maintenance responsibility – so keep things local unless you can guarantee that someone else will maintain your distant cache.

CREATING GEOCACHES

**Disguised cache containers: pine cone, bolt, mushroom**

The first golden rule is that you must think carefully about how your cache and the actions of fellow geocachers might be perceived by the public. A cache concealed in full view of offices or apartments, for example, risks geocachers being regarded as suspicious.

If in doubt, find another location – the UK has over 160,000 caches but there's still plenty of room. Popular locations include the base/roots of trees, among logs, under rocks, in crevices, under bridges (provided this can be accomplished safely), in bird feeders hanging from trees, and in a whole host of places if you're using magnetic containers. Much thought needs to go into choosing the right place; don't just select somewhere at random because it conveniently has a nice hidey-hole.

A concealed cache should not be easily visible to a passer-by. Use creativity and imagination to make a challenging concealment.

## CACHE SATURATION

You should not place caches in an area already well covered by caches. It's a requirement of www.geocaching.com that physical caches are separated by at least 0.1 miles (161m/528ft) in a direct line – although caches that lie on either side of a river, where the walk to each is greater than the prescribed distance, would be acceptable.

The aim of this requirement is to encourage the placing of caches in areas not already covered. Do not place caches every 530ft, just because you can. Be a little more

In public areas, avoid using containers that may appear suspicious, and do not secure them with wires or tape. To reduce confusion and alarm when a cache is discovered accidentally, clearly label your container on the outside with appropriate information to say it's a geocache and harmless. You can buy pre-printed labels to stick on the cache indicating that it's an official geocache and part of a game, so use these if you can, or improvise appropriately.

**Pre-printed labels for affixing to cache containers**

imaginative and earn yourself a reputation as a considerate geocache owner.

## PERMANENCE AND PERMISSION

You must remember that your cache needs a significant degree of permanence about it, so do not place caches that might disintegrate, be swept away by floodwater, fall from the hiding place, and so on.

You also need to ensure that you have the permission of the owner of the land on which the cache is placed before you hide the cache. Some organisations (listed in the Land Agreement database on www.gagb.org.uk), including the National Trust, the Woodland Trust and the Forestry Commission, give guidelines on their respective websites, but you will be asked to confirm when submitting your cache for review either that you've been given permission to place your cache, or that the landowner has given a blanket consent to geocaching. In some instances you'll need to apply to the landowner for consent to place a cache on their land. Several landowners, such as the Woodland Trust, have downloadable forms on their website for this purpose.

Bear in mind that geocaching is still a relatively new activity, and some landowners do not understand what it is; take the time to explain.

## WHERE NOT TO HIDE A CACHE

There are quite a few places where you should **not** conceal caches, and for your cache to be listed on www. geocaching.com it needs to meet certain criteria. Generally, caches should not be:

- **buried** – it's fine to cover a cache with branches, leaves, stones and rocks, but it's not acceptable to hide a cache by digging and burying it

Caches that take players to historical locations are always popular (this is Castle Bolton in North Yorkshire), but if you are placing a cache in such places, do be sure to get the landowner's permission first

- **within environmentally sensitive areas**, including nature reserves, sites of special scientific interest (SSSI), sites of biodiversity importance, archaeological sites, or any place where human activity might disturb wildlife. That's not to say that you can't place caches in these areas, but you will need permission from the landowner/manager
- **close to railway lines**, unless there's adequate fencing to prevent access to the lines
- anywhere that might cause **concern for public safety or about terrorist activity**, such as near airports, tunnels, bridges, military installations, local water supplies or government buildings

Urban caches should be placed to minimise the chance of security alerts. It's essential that micros and larger caches are marked externally as a geocache. Containers larger than 35mm canisters should have clear sides to enable inspection without opening.

### DETERMINING THE CO-ORDINATES

Once you've found the perfect place for a cache, you need to determine its co-ordinates as precisely as you can. First, remember to ensure that your GPS device is using the WGS84 datum, and that it's set to use degrees and decimal minutes (hddd*mm.mmm).

Getting accurate co-ordinates is probably the most difficult thing about placing a cache. There are many factors that can produce variations, and you may find that the co-ordinates change from minute to minute. If you're out in the open, the chances are that you'll get good satellite coverage and can therefore produce very good co-ordinates. But if your cache is in woodland, for example, it may not be so easy to get a clear reading. And there are certain times of day when satellite coverage is greater than at others; this will affect the accuracy, too.

To begin with, have your GPS device turned on as you approach the cache location. Then, as you reach the hiding place, note the co-ordinates. Now walk on by and turn round to come back, making another note of the co-ordinates. Do this a few times, and you can see which co-ordinates are the most likely to be accurate. (Note that some GPS devices have an averaging feature that compares co-ordinates at a single spot over a few minutes, and then averages the result.) If you're with someone else who has a GPS, get them to check the reading too.

Finally, once back home, you can check the co-ordinates on Google Earth. This is not always wholly reliable, and should not be used for calculating co-ordinates, but the clarity of Google Earth is often such that you can actually see the mound of rocks beneath which you placed the cache, and can compare the readings. If you get widely differing results, you may have to check the co-ordinates out in the field once more. If in doubt, use the figures on your GPS device.

## CACHE CONTENTS

Use common sense when choosing the contents. Explosives, fireworks, knives, drugs, alcohol and other illicit items should not be placed in a cache. Geocaching is a family activity and cache contents should be suitable for all ages.

Food items are always a bad idea, and in some cases caches have been chewed through and destroyed by animals because food items (or items that smell like food) are in the cache.

If the original cache contents lists questionable items, or if a cache is subsequently reported to contain questionable items, the cache may be disabled by the reviewers, and the owner of the cache contacted and asked to remove the items before the cache is enabled.

## CACHES THAT SOLICIT AND COMMERCIAL CACHES

Caches posted for religious, political, charitable or social reasons, or which solicit support for such causes, are not permitted. Geocaching is supposed to be a light, fun activity, and not to have a hidden agenda.

Commercial caches will not be published on www.geocaching.com without prior approval. A commercial cache is a geocache listing, or actual geocache, which is perceived to have been submitted with the principal or substantial

7

CREATING GEOCACHES

intent of soliciting customers or generating commercial gain. The geocache is presumed to be commercial if the finder is required to go inside a business, interact with employees, and/or purchase a product or service, or if the cache listing has overtones of advertising, marketing or promotion.

## SUBMITTING A GEOCACHE FOR REVIEW

Geocaching is a self-regulating activity, but one that adheres to a number of guidelines. To ensure that you've followed those guidelines, a team of 'reviewers' will look at the details of your proposed cache before it can be published on www.geocaching.com. In order to submit a cache you will have to indicate that you've read and understood the extensive guidelines on listing requirements. During the review process, a reviewer checks the page for inaccuracies, poor co-ordinates and compliance with the guidelines. If the reviewer has any reservations about your cache, he/she will temporarily disable the cache pending clarification.

One of the principal reasons for a cache not being published is its proximity to other caches (see 'Cache saturation', above). It's easy to check the whereabouts of traditional caches, because their location is on the website. But, unless you tackle all the multi-caches in the area, you won't know the location of any final or bonus caches, and they may be close to your intended place. If they are, the reviewer will let you know. As part of the submission process, a page will display visible locations that are already taken by existing caches.

This image shows the visible locations of existing geocaches in the area

It's a requirement that your cache should already be in place before you submit it for review. From one point of view this is odd, because if it's not published you'll have to go out again and retrieve the cache. From another point of view, requiring the cache to be in place is vital because it becomes live the moment the reviewer publishes it, and therefore needs to be in place. Some geocachers like to compete to be

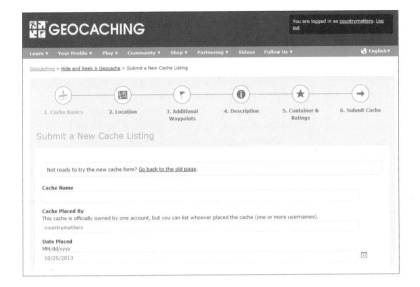

**The start of the New Cache Listing page, which has six stages to complete up to final submission**

the 'First to find' (FTF) new caches, so your cache has to be there for them to find from the outset, even if it's published late at night. Some geocachers go out with torches!

## THE REVIEW PROCESS

Begin the review process by selecting 'Play' from the top menu on the home page. Then choose 'Hide and seek a cache'. This takes you to a two-part page, with 'Hide a cache' on the right. Within this panel is a link to 'Start Cache Submission Process; you should select this to be redirected to a page headed 'Hide a Geocache'. This is what you are now going to do, so select 'Continue'.

There are a number of fields on the next page. Each will contribute to the finished cache page, but some aspects of page design may need you to go back to make adjustments before you're happy with the finished page. If you understand how to use html coding you may want to select 'Go back to the old page', the layout of which is slightly different, but which allows you to use html to design your page.

- **Cache name** – this is where you give the cache a name. Think of something imaginative and relevant to the location. If you're entering more than one cache as part of a series, begin with the series name, such as 'White Cliffs of Dover: Lighthouse'.
- **Cache placed by** – this is where you enter your geocaching pseudonym.
- **Date placed** – this will default to the current date, but can be adjusted if you don't want the cache to go live until a later date.

Further down the page you need to select the '**Cache Type**'. Then tick the two boxes at the bottom, and select 'Continue'.

The next page begins 'Let's work on the location of your Traditional cache', and asks you to **enter the cache co-ordinates and its location** in the UK. The regional choices here are limited, so be sure to get the right one. After that you have the chance to enter any **additional waypoints** you might want to include, such as the co-ordinates for car parking. You don't have to complete this section, but it's always helpful to show where visitors can park.

Now you get to the longer pages, which ask you to enter:

- **Cache summary** – which is just that. It is intended to give location information, along with notes on the terrain and general difficulty levels, and is limited to 500 characters.

- **Cache description** – there is no character limit on this field, and here you should impart information about the cache. This is where you 'sell' the cache to other geocachers; include historical, wildlife, landscape, architectural and other notes – in fact anything that makes the

*Canal towpaths and adjacent land make excellent locations for cache concealment*

cache interesting. You can enter the information using html coding, but this is not essential. The key point is to tell geocachers what your cache is about, and why it's placed where it is.

In both of the above sections you have the opportunity to design the cache page yourself, to include hyperlinks (possibly giving background information about the location) and to add pictures. It's worth taking time to look closely at the wide range of choices available, and before completing the page you might want to put your text into something like Microsoft Word and run a spell check. This will rectify any silly mistakes and potentially save embarrassment. The reviewers do not alter your text – that's your job.

- **Hints** – it's for you to decide whether or not to include a hint. Any hints about the location of the cache will be encrypted. How much information you give, and how cryptic the message, is up to you. You can be fairly explicit – 'Under stile beside fence' – or a little obtuse – 'Lowly, bolely, holey'. Giving hints is a skill in itself. Wait until you've tried finding caches without using a hint and you'll understand; you'll also see what level of clue you need to give. Something a little bit out of the ordinary is quite acceptable – it makes searchers think. But at the end of the day you want your cache to be found, so think carefully about your hints. The hint should not reveal the location of the cache, but should give a good clue as to where it can be found.

- **Background image** – enables you to change the background image on the web page to a location of your choosing.

- **Related web page** – if you've created a separate web page relating to the cache, or there's already a site-specific web page, this is the place to enter the URL (website address).

It's on this page that you also decide whether to make your cache available to everyone, or just to Premium members. Choosing to make them available to Premium members reduces the risk of caches being destroyed by non-geocachers who've stumbled upon them chance. But it also eliminates the cache from the view of genuine beginners.

Continuing across the pages, you're next asked to select the **size** of your cache container. 'Not chosen' is the selection normally reserved for geocaching events, while 'Other' might be used for a cache that's not a container in the normal sense – you'll know one when you find one.

- **Overall difficulty rating** – this is where you grade the difficulty of your cache in increments of half a point. For this, and the terrain rating below, there's a sub-system that allows you to enter information about your cache, and this will generate a suggested rating for it. You don't have to accept it, but entries that give inaccurate ratings are misleading, so you may want to be guided by the system. Unlike terrain rating (below), assessing difficulty differs according to the type of cache. At present, there's no system for distinguishing between caches that are simply difficult to find and those that involve solving puzzles, which, of course vary according to your ability to solve the puzzle. Difficulty rating tends to relate to the ease with which the puzzle might be solved (subjective), rather than the ease of finding it (objective).

- **Overall terrain rating**: the terrain rating indicates how easy it is to get to the cache location. Anything rated 2 or less is generally accepted as being accessible by wheelchairs and buggies. The highest grade (5) should be reserved for the most difficult terrain or ascents of mountains (the cache on the summit of Ben More on the Isle of Mull – GCTFPZ – is rated 5 for terrain as it's a long climb from sea level, but the difficulty rating is only 2.5). If you're uncertain, use the in-built system to see what rating the website suggests, and use this as a guide. The author uses a personal guide that grades terrain according to the ability of less-abled geocachers to negotiate it, incrementally up to a 3, beyond which the terrain is regarded as too difficult for wheelchairs or less-abled people. But this is a purely personal approach. It may also be that the greater part of an approach to a cache is no more than a 2, but a final slope or a move around a rocky edge with a steep drop can elevate the grade, and it's this final section that earns the overall grade (see GC51GNZ – Mull: Duart Point).
- **Attributes** – the symbols used to denote 'attributes' tell you what to expect at a cache location. Cache owners can identify search attributes for their cache covering:
  - **permissions** – whether dogs are allowed, for example
  - **conditions** – walking time involved, suitability for children, whether the cache is available at all times, and so on
  - **special equipment** – money (for a parking fee, say), a torch or climbing equipment

- **hazards** – such as thorns or dangerous terrain
- **facilities** – accessibility for wheelchairs, availability of parking, public transport, and so on.
- Premium members can run a search known as a 'Pocket Query' (see Chapter 9) to search for caches with particular attributes.

- **Note to reviewer** – in order to speed up the publishing process you need to provide details of your cache that will help the reviewer. The reviewer deletes the note before your cache is published, although if you access your listing in the meantime – perhaps to edit it – then the note to reviewer will appear. In this section you need to explain that you have permission to place the cache where it is, or otherwise give information that will help the reviewer to publish it quickly. If the reviewer has any concerns about your cache, he/she will contact you and explain what those concerns are to give you a chance to amend the listing or provide further information. This is normal procedure and it applies to everyone.

Finally, you'll be required to 'Save and Exit' and wait.

**Under a stone!**

CREATING GEOCACHES

In the meantime you can continue to edit your listing, if you realise that you've made a mistake or want to clarify something. There's an immediate option to edit your listing as soon as you submit it – the page is self-explanatory. But if you have second thoughts a little later, select 'Your profile' from the home page of the website, and directly above any 'Recently viewed caches' or 'Your logs (Last 30 days)' you'll find your pending caches – 'Unpublished Disabled Caches' – as a list. You can access them and make changes by using the 'Edit listing' option in the Navigation panel.

## MAINTAINING A GEOCACHE

There's nothing worse than finding a cache that is not maintained and is left to deteriorate – there's no fun in that!

The process of placing a geocache carries with it the considerable responsibility of maintaining the cache, which is a good reason for not placing caches too far from your home. In fact, if the reviewer notices that your cache is a long way from your home co-ordinates, and you haven't made any arrangement with a local geocacher to maintain it, the cache may well not be published.

You should plan on visiting your cache from time to time to check on its condition, and it's important to do so as soon as possible after receiving an online log entry indicating that the cache needs maintenance. Often it may involve nothing more than replacing a full logbook, but caches do become waterlogged, either through direct water penetration or by condensation, and it's your responsibility to 'repair' whatever damage has been caused. Occasionally you may need to replace the entire cache container with a new one.

When you visit your cache, check that the area around it is not becoming trampled by geocachers searching for it and creating paths leading to it. If necessary, consider relocating your cache or permanently removing it. If you take either of these actions, remember to post a note on the cache page of the website. If you do permanently remove a cache you should also remember to archive it (one of the options available to the cache owner): this makes your cache inactive so people don't go searching for something that's no longer there.

Whenever someone finds, or doesn't find, your cache, you'll receive an email to that effect. Be sure to read the log entries – they can alert you to the need to carry out maintenance.

### Maintenance guidelines

The www.geocaching.com guidelines specify that 'As the cache owner, you are responsible for physically checking your cache periodically, and especially when someone reports a problem with the cache (for example it is missing, damaged or wet). You may temporarily disable your cache

## RESPONDING TO A 'NEEDS MAINTENANCE' NOTE

Should you receive a 'Needs maintenance' email, you have a responsibility to deal with it. The fact that someone has flagged the cache as being in need of attention is shown by a red spanner icon, and this remains against the cache until it is cleared. Moreover, the cache that needs maintenance appears in a list presented to you as a reminder, should you decide to place new caches elsewhere.

You can clear the 'Needs maintenance' icon only by performing 'Owner maintenance', which results in a green spanner icon and the clearance of the cache from any list identifying those in need of maintenance. Once you've attended to the maintenance, simply go to the cache page, select 'Log your visit' and then select 'Owner maintenance' from the drop-down list.

to let others know not to hunt for it until you have a chance to fix the problem. This feature is to allow you a reasonable time – normally a few weeks – in which to arrange a visit to your cache. In the event that a cache is not being properly maintained, or has been temporarily disabled for an extended period of time, the listing may be archived.'

## PUTTING A CACHE UP FOR ADOPTION

Occasionally you may not be able to maintain your own caches – perhaps you're moving away from the area, for example. But it's essential that caches are always properly maintained, so if you find yourself in this position you need to put your caches up for adoption by a local geocacher.

The way you do this will depend on how well you know your local geocaching community. It's unlikely that you'll find no-one willing to take over your caches, but if all else fails you can try writing a note into the relevant cache pages, saying you're looking for someone to adopt your cache(s). Once you find someone who's willing to take over your caches, go to www.geocaching.com/adopt and enter the code of the cache you're putting up for adoption. This will take you through to a page on which you enter the username of the person who's adopting your cache. When finished, click on 'Send adoption request', and the system does the rest.

If the process is being done in reverse and you're adopting someone else's caches, then when you receive notification that the cache has been transferred to you it's courtesy to acknowledge the transfer somewhere on the cache page in one of the description panels.

## DELETING LOG ENTRIES AND IMAGES

Very occasionally, log entries may be inappropriate; in such cases, as cache owner you can delete them. Go to 'Your profile' and select 'Geocaches (Yours)'. Select the cache in question and scroll down to the log entries. Find the offending log and select 'View log'. You'll then find the page 'View Geocache Log', on which you can select 'Delete log'. Of course, this should be used only as a last resort, and it may be worth contacting the person who wrote the log and asking them to change it.

You can also delete any images that you feel give away the cache location.

## CREATING AN EARTHCACHE

All EarthCaches are subject to the normal review process, but because they don't have a physical cache container, and are intended to serve a different purpose from conventional caches, there's an additional set of guidelines for those wanting to create caches of this type:

- EarthCaches must provide an Earth science lesson.
- EarthCaches must be educational. They provide accurate, educational, but non-technical explanations of what visitors will experience at the site. The cache page, including the description and logging tasks, must assume only a basic knowledge of geology.
- EarthCaches must highlight a unique feature. EarthCaches that duplicate existing EarthCache information about the site or related sites may be rejected. EarthCaches must be developed to provide a unique experience to the location's visitors, and to teach a unique lesson about the feature at the site. Multiple EarthCaches on the same feature should be avoided and content, rather than proximity, will be the guiding principle of EarthCache reviewers.
- EarthCaches must have approval from the Land Manager prior to submission (depending on local laws and customs). The name, title and contact details of the person that authorised the EarthCache must be included in a Reviewer Note. Otherwise, information about the type of land, and the reasons why permission may not be required, must be included in a Reviewer Note.
- An EarthCache can be a single site or multiple sites. You must have visited the site(s) recently (within two months) to make current, first-hand observations. You must provide accurate coordinates for each site where

visitors are to perform the logging tasks, and ensure these areas are accessible to the public. You are responsible for taking appropriate actions if conditions change regarding access, permission, or other concerns.

- Logging an EarthCache requires visitors to undertake a site-specific task which provides a learning opportunity related to the topic. The logging tasks must have visitors using the information from the cache page along with their observations at the site to perform some type of analysis of their own. Logging task solutions will serve as the cache owner's proof that the cacher has visited the site. Questions which only serve to prove that someone visited the site, and do not relate to the site's geology, are not permitted. All requests for photographs must be optional. Visitors must be able to send their answers to logging tasks via the cache owner's profile. Auto-responders cannot be used to verify answers. The answers to the logging tasks must be placed in a Reviewer Note at the time of submission.

- The EarthCache text and logging tasks must be submitted in the local language. Additional languages are encouraged, but the local language must be listed first. You may be requested to provide text in a language understandable to your reviewer to assist with the reviewing process.

- Respect Trademarks and Copyright and only use text, images or logos if you have permission. EarthCaches with information that is copied from other sources, plagiarized, or used without proper attribution will not be published. Limited amounts of text may be quoted, but must be properly attributed.

- EarthCache sites adhere to the principles of geocaching and Leave No Trace outdoor ethics. In addition, use waypoints to ensure cachers take appropriate pathways and use established trails only. Damage to the site is unacceptable. Please be mindful of fragile ecosystems. EarthCache sites will highlight the principle of collect memories – not samples. Furthermore, no physical cache, or other items, can be left at the site.

- EarthCaches are submitted through www.geocaching. com and must meet these guidelines and adhere to the Geocache Listing Requirements/Guidelines and www. geocaching.com Site Terms of Use Agreement. The Geological Society of America and the EarthCache Team retains the right to edit, modify, reject or archive any EarthCache that does not adhere to these guidelines, or for any other purpose that the Team deems as appropriate.

Castle Ewen in the Fairy Glen, Isle of Skye, makes a perfect EarthCache

# 8 TRACKABLE ITEMS

As you discover more and more caches you will inevitably encounter what are known as trackable items. These take two forms: Travel bugs and geocoins. Images of geocoins are dotted throughout these pages.

The purpose of trackable items (also known as 'hitch-hikers' and 'travellers') is for them to be transported from cache to cache, usually in accordance with some basic idea – such as 'to visit mountain caches', 'to travel the world', 'to visit every country', 'to travel around national parks', and so on. It is for the owners of trackable items to assign a purpose. In reality, most owners keep it simple – 'to travel to as many caches as possible' – but there are some more difficult requirements to comply with – 'to visit caches at surfing beaches', 'to visit caches that begin with the letter R' (for example), or 'to visit caches beginning with successive letters of the alphabet'. When a trackable item is picked up from a cache, the finder logs it on the website and, later, records where it's dropped off, so that 'owners' can track these items on their journey.

A geocoin (one example of the many colourful designs scattered throughout this book)

> Finding and moving on trackable items is an exciting and fascinating part of geocaching, especially when you find one that has travelled the world many times over. Geocoins, in particular, are of outstanding design and have become collectable items. Not that you should keep any you find in caches: that is not in the spirit of geocaching.

## TRAVEL BUGS®

A Travel bug, usually abbreviated to 'TB', takes the basic form of a two-part dog tag with a unique reference number. Owners of TBs will usually attach something (anything reasonable) to the tag, such as a golf ball, key ring, toy car, doll, or even junk cleared out from caches.

Travel bug tags (this is a dummy – tracking numbers should never be disclosed)

### Picking up a Travel bug

There is no obligation to remove a TB from a cache; you can simply note its number and then 'Discover' it on the TB's home page. But most people do take them, with the intention of moving them on. If you do pick up a TB, record this on the website as follows:

- Locate the unique tracking number, which is stamped on the dog tag. If you are intending to move the trackable on immediately (before returning home from your geocaching trip), make a note of this number so that you can record what you've done online later.
- Once back at your computer, select 'Find trackables' from the top drop-down menu and enter the unique number in the 'Enter tracking code of the item' field. Then select 'Track' to go through to the TB's own page.
- At the TB's page, select 'Found it? Log it' from the Trackable Options panel.
- Select 'Post a new log' in the same way you would after finding a cache (the tracking code is automatically carried through from the earlier page). Now write some comments so that the owner knows where the trackable is and what's happening to it. You don't have to say much, but it's always welcome if you do. For example, you could explain the circumstances of the find.
- Once you've completed this process you'll find that the name of the trackable has been added to an inventory at the bottom of the right-hand panel on the 'Your profile' page. This is 'Your inventory', and it contains a list of trackable items currently in your possession.

Bear in mind that trackable items are meant to be moved on, and you should endeavour to do so within a period of two weeks. If it's likely to take longer than this, you should contact the owner as a matter of courtesy and let them know when you hope to move the item on.

**A well-travelled travel bug, with post-box attachment**

### Missing trackables

From time to time you'll find that TBs listed in the inventory on a cache page are not present in the cache container. There are a number of possible reasons for this:

- Someone got to it ahead of you and has yet to record that it's been retrieved – this often happens when that person is on holiday without access to the internet.
- It was never there in the first place; the previous 'finder' entered the information on the wrong cache page.
- It's been stolen, usually by a muggle, but sometimes – if it was a particularly attractive TB – by a geocacher not playing the game. Activated TBs do occasionally turn up on online auction sites.

### Dropping off a Travel bug

Once you've logged your retrieval of a TB you can physically drop it off into another cache. As you're logging your visit to the cache in which you've placed the TB, go to the bottom of the page and locate the TB you've left. Click on the box at the right of this panel and select 'Dropped off', then select 'Submit your log entry'. If you forget to log the TB drop you can always edit your log entry or 'Write a note' saying something like 'TB drop'. You also have the option simply to 'Visit' the trackable to a particular cache: many trackables are entered into races between geocachers to see how far the item can travel in a year, or how many caches they can visit. So, dipping them into caches, or 'Visiting' them, adds to the overall distance travelled. But you will have to give it up sooner or later and drop it into a cache.

If the TB has a purpose or goal, try to comply with it as closely as possible. For example, if the goal is to take the TB to the seaside, don't leave it on a mountain; if it wants to go north, don't take it south. If you realise that you can't comply with the TB's mission, then either put it back where you found it or place it in a cache that might help it on its way – for example, a TB that wants to visit Australia could be dropped in a cache on the way to an airport.

### Your own Travel bugs

When you buy a new dog-tag TB – they are available online at many outlets – it comes in two parts. One is the travelling tag and the other is the owner's, marked as a 'Copy'. Both are the owner's property. It's unusual for unattached dog tags alone to be left in caches; more commonplace is for the owner to attach an object that can be used to give the TB a sense of purpose. These range from small key rings to golf balls, teddy bears, toy dogs, toy cars... anything, in fact, that lends a little interest to the items.

Each dog tag is stamped with a unique tracking number, by which the item is identified. But before you can do anything with it, the tag must be activated – a simple process.

### Activating a Travel bug
- Select 'Find trackables' from the drop-down menu on the www.geocaching.com home page.
- On the 'Trackables' page, enter the unique reference number in the field marked 'Activate trackable items', then select 'Activate'.
- You will next be asked to enter an activation code; this appears on or in the packet containing the Travel bug. Enter the activation code and select 'Activate your trackable item'.
- The website automatically generates a TB reference number, which is not the same as the tracking number

Black Rock Cottage along the West Highland Way is the location of a popular traditional cache

on the actual TB. The reference number (also known as the TB number) can easily be confused with the number on the dog tag. The TB number is the code on each TB's page, which is the 'safe' number to help users reference each TB without giving out the bug's actual tracking number.

- You can give the TB a name, or you can just leave it as 'Travel bug dog tag' and assign a mission to it. What do you want it to do? It could visit mountains, railway stations, parks, waterfalls… and so on. It makes sense to prescribe a mission that's easily achieved, and which therefore generates a history worth following, rather than simply a mission to visit South Africa or Australia. Such missions are possible, but unless your TB is discovered by someone who's going there, it's unlikely to arrive. If, however, the TB does reach South Africa or Australia, its mission is then complete and the TB technically redundant, so don't forget to add '…and then come home.'

- Finally, enter a brief description of the tag and anything you may attach to it. Select 'Edit trackable item's description', and on the next page complete the fields marked 'Location activated', then select 'Complete activation'.

- Activation is now complete, and your trackable item has its own home page.

### Keeping tabs on your TB

Once you've placed your TB in a cache, sit back and wait to see if anyone finds it and moves it on. When someone does log a find, you'll receive an email telling you so.

On 'Your profile' page, select 'Trackables (Yours)'. This takes you to a 'Search trackable items' page, where all your own trackable items are listed. You can see at a glance where your trackable is currently located, and, in the right-hand column, how far it has travelled since you originally placed it.

Click on one of the trackable names and you are taken to the individual page for that item – one that shows the history of your item, who found it, who moved it and to where. The line 'Tracking history' gives the distance the item has travelled. Select 'View map' and the item's journeys are illustrated on a world map.

There are a number of websites that allow you to keep a track of your trackables. However, they do occasionally go missing; in this case you need to visit the relevant page for your trackable and mark it as missing. It will then be removed from your trackable inventory.

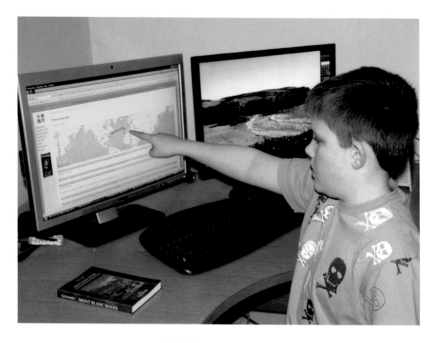

Following the journeys of a trackable item are a good way of generating a world geography lesson for young children (and adults, too)

## GEOCOINS

A geocoin is a special coin created by individuals or groups of geocachers as a 'signature item' or 'calling card'; many of them are associated with geocaching events. Like TBs, each geocoin is assigned a unique tracking number, which allows them to travel from cache to cache or to be passed among friends, picking up stories along the way.

### Picking up and dropping off geocoins

The procedure for picking up geocoins from caches, and for ensuring their onward travel, is exactly the same as for TBs.

### Discovery

One of the options you have on finding either a TB or a geocoin is to leave it where it is and simply 'Discover' it. This means that you're recording the fact that you found it, but didn't take it. You'll find that this option becomes available to you on the 'Found it? Log it' page.

### Collecting geocoins

The design of most geocoins is quite stunning, and not surprisingly they've become collectors' items. But, since activated geocoins are the trackable property of the owner, they are not yours for the keeping. You must 'play the game' and move them on. If you want to collect geocoins there are many available for purchase on the internet.

Typical geocoins

### Tracking your geocoins
You can track your geocoins in exactly the same way that you track a TB (see above).

### 'MOBILE' TRACKABLE ITEMS
To extend the 'discovery' element of trackable items, it's possible to acquire magnetic or adhesive TBs that you can affix to items such as your car, so turning it into a mobile TB – although you should make it clear on the TB's page that it's not for moving on (see 1PHA7P: XC70). Alternatively, you could fasten TBs to your key ring or wear them as jewellery. When you find a mobile TB, simply make a note of its code and then log your 'discovery' of it. The author often wears a trackable t-shirt to event caches; it has a valid tracking number and so can be 'discovered'.

8

A stunning dolerite sill intrusion EarthCache at Rubh' an Dunain, Isle of Skye

# MORE ADVANCED STUFF

Groundspeak is the parent company for geocaching; it's a privately held company based in Seattle, Washington. The company evolved almost immediately after the US government turned off selective availability on its GPS satellites in May 2000, and the first cache was placed within 24hrs. Within three days, two others had used their GPS devices to locate the cache; during the following week more did the same, and geocaching was born.

The building of the www.geocaching.com website was to come within four months, dedicated to the role location-based technology could play in outdoor recreation. When the website was launched in September 2000 there were just 75 caches worldwide. At the time of writing (June 2014), there are 2,415,780 – double the number quoted in the first edition of this book.

**GEOCACHING.COM**

## BENEFITS OF PREMIUM MEMBERSHIP

To use www.geocaching.com you have to become a member, and there are two levels of membership available. The **basic level** of membership, which is free, allows you to:

- view co-ordinates and location information for geocaches
- write about your finds and your experiences on the website.
- In addition, **premium membership**, which costs $30 a year (2014), gives access to website features and functionality that will enhance your geocaching experience. These include:
- organising your favourites – you can create 'favourites' lists, such as dog-friendly caches or puzzle caches, using a Bookmark feature (see 'Manage bookmarks', below)
- creating custom searches – downloading up to 1000 waypoints, based on cache size, location, attributes, and so on – using Pocket Queries (see below)
- searching for geocaches along a particular route
- accessing other related websites, including www.waymarking.com and www.whereigo.com
- receiving Instant Notifications of new caches to enable you to be the First To Find (FTF).

## GROUNDSPEAK NEWSLETTER

Groundspeak issue a weekly newsletter containing informa-tion about forthcoming Mega-events, news items and gen-eral events. There's a strong US element, but the section on 'Upcoming events' is especially useful to geocachers in the UK.

Also listed are recent additions to the cache database; these are based on your home co-ordinates and therefore feature caches close to where you live.

## YOUR ACCOUNT DETAILS

The page listing your account details is where you provide basic information about yourself. Some of the information is, by default, not public; other information is limited, by you, to just that degree of information you wish to disclose.

You can access your account details most easily by selecting 'Your profile' from the website home page top menu. Then select 'Your account details'. This includes key information about your account with Groundspeak, allows you to upload a photograph of yourself, and gives details of your membership and the date of renewal, along with the email address you're using with www.geocaching.com and other preferences of your choice.

## YOUR PUBLIC PROFILE

The page displaying 'Your public profile' is accessed through the right-hand column on 'Your profile' page – just above the number of 'Finds' and 'Hides' you have made. This is what anyone using www.geocaching.com will see about you. It tells people how long you've been a member, enables them to send you an email message, and includes a section on profile information, the contents of which are entirely at your discretion. You edit the profile information shown on this page by selecting the 'Edit your profile' link near the top of the page.

Your profile also lists other information:

- **Geocaches** – by selecting the page for 'Geocaches' from within your profile page, you're shown the total number and types of caches you've found, along with any you've created. Select 'All geocache finds' and you'll be shown several pages listing all the caches you've found, starting with the most recent. Similarly, if you select 'All geocache hides' you'll be shown a list of all the caches you've created.
- **Trackables** – select 'Trackables' from your profile page and you'll be shown a list of all the trackable items you've discovered or moved on. It also shows any trackables that you own.

'Barnaby in the wild' –
geocaching is a great way
to encourage children to
appreciate our countryside
(photo: Mark Fishwick)

- **Souvenirs** – these are virtual pieces of art that can be discovered and displayed on your profile page. They're linked to a specific location or event, and may be linked by time also. If, for example, you attend an event for which Groundspeak has published a souvenir (in August 2013 they had one for every day of the month), and it's part of a challenge, the souvenir is automatically added to your profile page.
- **Gallery** – this page shows any photographs you've uploaded to the various cache pages on the website.
- **Lists** – this page lists any caches you may have inserted in a bookmarked list you've produced and saved using Pocket Queries.
- **Statistics** – this page gives much fascinating information about your activities as a geocacher, including your 'Finds per month', 'Yearly breakdown', 'Finds for each day of the year' (the Day Grid), 'Cache types', 'Difficulty and Terrain of caches found' (the D/T grid), and much more. Of particular note are the maps of where you've found caches and particular milestones in your geocaching career.

When you first select 'Your profile' from the home page you're shown an abbreviated list of all your 'Finds' and 'Hides'. By selecting 'Geocaches' from the top menu on this page you're taken to an expanded version of the geocaches you've logged, including your log entry in full. The same is true when you select 'Trackable items'.

Next to each of these links appears '(Yours)'; if you select these you're taken to pages displaying your own caches (those you've created) and your own trackable items (any that you've placed and which are originally yours).

These pages enable you to quickly visit your own cache pages, view comments or make changes to the listing.

## POCKET QUERIES

Only premium members have access to Pocket Queries. Pocket Queries (PQs) use a system of filters that enable you to search through the database in a specific way, and to have search results emailed to you on a regular basis, or as a one-off exercise. PQs can be especially helpful in planning geocaching trips; using them, you can receive information on as many as 1000 caches all at one time, and many of the modern GPS devices are enabled to accept direct downloads such as these. You can search for caches that meet certain criteria – such as 'Dog friendly' or 'Recommended for children' – or caches of a certain type or size, or within a certain distance of your home or destination. This system also allows you to update the status of any caches you've downloaded so that you can avoid going out in search of caches that have disappeared or been archived.

### Creating Pocket Queries

The procedure for creating Pocket Queries is lengthy (see below), but not overly complex. Even so, the use of PQs is something you may want to delay until you have a good understanding of everything that geocaching involves. In this way, you can maximise the benefits that accrue from the use of PQs.

- In the drop-down menu under 'Your profile', select 'Pocket Queries'. This takes you to a page headed 'Your Pocket Queries' – one that retains and lists any PQs you make, until you decide to delete them.
- Select 'Create a new query'.
- On the page headed 'New Pocket Query', give your query a name (such as 'Trackables near home') – something by which you can retrieve it from among any subsequent queries you may create.
- Choose the day of the week on which you want to receive the results of the query. If you don't select a day, the query won't run. The usual thing is to select the current day.
- For queries that you want to run on a regular basis, decide how often you would like the query to run. **Note** 'Uncheck the day of the week after the query runs'

enables you to run a query once, and then save it in your list of queries for later use. The other options are to run the query every week on the days you select, or simply to run the query once and then delete it. You might want to run a weekly query if you live in an area of high cache density and where new caches are published frequently.

- Enter the number of cache listings you'd like to receive – 1000 is the maximum, 500 is the default setting.
- If you want listings of all types of cache, leave 'Any type' selected – or you can filter the results by selecting different options.
- If you leave 'Any container' selected you'll get all geocache listings, but you can filter these selectively.
- Under 'That (And)', leave all boxes unchecked except 'I haven't found', 'I don't own' and 'Is enabled' if you want to receive all live caches, or choose some options to filter the final list.
- Under 'And' you can determine the Difficulty and Terrain rating of caches you want to find. To receive caches for all levels of difficulty or terrain, leave the ratings unchecked. Of course, you can select any level of difficulty or terrain.
- 'Within' can be left as 'None selected'.
- Under 'From origin', select the option that gives you the best centre point of the location where you would like to search. You can then enter the radius to delimit an area within which you want to search. The customary choices are 'My home location' or 'By co-ordinates'. In the latter case, you have to enter the relevant coordinates; the best approach here is to find a cache on the Geocaching.com Map that's in the centre of the area you're searching and use the co-ordinates for that cache, then set the radius. This is particularly useful if you want all the caches over a wide area. For example, to list all the caches on the Isle of Man, select a cache in the centre of the island and set the radius at 30km; this will embrace all the caches on the island.
- The greatest number of results will come by leaving 'Placed during' and 'Attributes' unchecked.
- Choose the format in which you want to receive the details. GPX results will give more information, including hints and logs; LOC format gives only co-ordinates. It is recommended that you select 'Compress files into *.zip format'; GPX and LOC files are text files, and compress very small and download more quickly. However, to use the .zip format you'll need software that will unzip the files, such as WinZip.

- Select 'Submit information' – the PQ results will be sent to you by email. It may not be an instant response, as the process depends on a dedicated computer handling hundreds of similar requests simultaneously.
- Once you've submitted the information, a 'Preview the search' link appears at the top of the page, on which you can see the results of your search. If you want to make changes to the results – by widening or reducing the search area, for example – then select 'Edit' from the top of the preview page. At this stage, by selecting 'Map this Location' you'll see a map on which you can verify that the query has covered the area you want.

### POCKET QUERY TIPS

- Queries are generated according to Pacific Standard Time (PST), which is 8hrs behind Greenwich Mean Time (GMT-8). This means that if you generate a query to be produced on a certain day, it could be up to 8hrs before the query runs. What may be Monday in the UK may still be Sunday at Groundspeak HQ.
- The more caches you choose, the larger your query file will be.
- Because you're limited to 1000 caches, in areas densely covered by caches consider using filters to create queries for different types of cache.
- Check how many caches can be loaded into your GPS, and don't request more than its limit.
- Eliminate caches that you know you're not likely to seek (such as multi- or mystery caches) if you're pressed for time.
- Start with one simple search to see how the system works before creating more.
- Be sure not to create searches that can't work, such as EarthCaches with trackable items.

### Using Pocket Queries to bulk download cache information

Use a combination of a bookmark list and a PQ, or just a PQ, to generate a GPX file of your search area. Then, using software such as EasyGPS (available free from www.easygps.com), open the GPX file, which will display all the caches in the file. Then connect your GPS to your computer and 'Send' the caches to it. This happens very quickly, but note that if the caches are some distance from your home location, they do not appear on your GPS until it's re-started

within the search area. For example, a file of caches for France will not appear until your GPS locates that it's in France.

**All sorts of toys are used to create geocaches**

## DISCOVER CACHES ALONG A ROUTE

If you're planning to make a long car journey, you can create a query that'll find caches along the route, allowing you to stop off and search for caches as you go. Of course, this prolongs the journey immensely, but it does make it more interesting. However, the system is highway oriented, and although it can be amended to include deviations, or should there be two or more possible routes between the start and finish points, it doesn't follow public footpaths, and so can't be used for cross-country routes.

The option to 'Find caches along a route' is available only to Premium members, and appears on the 'Your Pocket Queries' page. The resultant 'Find User Routes Near Your Trip' page has a number of options that allow you to 'Search for Existing Routes' (if you've already created routes); 'Search by Keyword'; 'Create a New Route'; and 'Upload a Route'.

Select 'Create a New Route' and give your route a name in the 'Enter Route Name' field, then select 'Create Route'.

9

Geocaching is a great family occasion

On the 'Create/Edit a Route' page the simplest way onward is to enter the 'From' and 'To' information in the relevant fields and then select 'Search'. Note that the route is limited to 500 miles (800km).

Once you've selected 'Search', you're shown a Google Map depicting your route. Now select 'Save route changes' at the bottom of the page and you're taken through to a 'Route information' page, in which you can give the route a name, enter a description of the route (along with any associated keywords) and then save it. If you tick the box 'Include in public directory', the route is made available for anyone to view.

Other options include 'Modify route' and 'Create a Pocket Query'. Selecting the latter generates a PQ as described above. 'Create GPX of Route' does just that: it creates a GPX file of your route (but only of your route – not of the caches along it).

Once you've created a route you can save it, and then revisit it later by selecting 'Find routes' from the right-hand menu under 'User Routes' on 'Your profile' page.

## MANAGE BOOKMARKS

A bookmark list can be used to list caches you want to find, to manage your Watchlist, to organise those caches you have found, to create a list of caches that may be part of a series that others can follow, and much more. You can keep the bookmark list private or share it with others.

A bookmark list can be most useful if you're undertaking, for example, a long-distance trail and you want to pick up caches along the route. But equally, you can compile a list of, say, your favourite caches, the most difficult caches you encountered, the most remote caches, and so on, and upload them for others to enjoy. Or you can just create a list of caches you intend to search for on any one given day – after which the list is deleted.

### Create a bookmark list
There are a few stages involved in creating a bookmark list, so be sure you want to do it before you make a start.
- From the 'Your profile' drop-down menu, select 'Lists'.
- On the 'List Management' page, select 'Create new bookmark list'.
- On the next page, give your list a name and enter a brief description of the list. Decide/select whether this list is for your personal use only (select none of the tick boxes), or will be viewable by others, in which case select 'I want to share this list with others' or 'Make this list public'. Then select 'Create bookmark list'.
- Now you've created a bookmark list, but as yet there's nothing in it. So, go to the first of the caches you want

Anyone concealing a cache in locations like this must respect the property and avoid damage (photo: Mark Fishwick)

117

Counting steps, as here at South Stack lighthouse, Holyhead, to give numeric information to complete cache co-ordinates is not everyone's favourite

to bookmark, and on the cache page select 'Bookmark' from the Navigation panel.

- The next page allows you to 'Create a bookmark', but be sure to put it in the correct list (from a drop-down menu) if you've created more than one bookmark list.
- Now simply repeat the process until all the caches you want to list are bookmarked. **Note** You can add caches to a bookmark list more quickly by using the Geocaching.com Map; clicking on the icon for the caches and selecting 'Bookmark it' from the small information panel that appears.
- Return to 'List management' from the top menu of 'Your profile' page, and you'll be taken through to a page with all your bookmarks listed.
- Select the one you're looking for and click on the hyperlink in the 'Name' column. This shows all the caches in that particular bookmark, and you can now generate a Pocket Query by selecting 'Create Pocket Query'. Equally, from 'Your Bookmark Lists' you can simply select 'Create Pocket Query' from the sixth column.

As a final move in this procedure, from your bookmarks list select 'Download GoogleEarth KML' (seventh column – see Chapter 4). This will download Google Earth and overlay on it the locations of all the caches in your bookmark.

## INSTANT NOTIFICATIONS

This facility allows you to receive notifications of new caches – in particular of event caches near you, but also of caches by type. This is especially useful if all you want to look for are, for example, EarthCaches.

### Set up Instant Notifications

- From 'Your profile' page, select 'Set up notifications' from the right-hand menu. Then, on the 'Instant Notification Service' page, select 'Create a new notification'.
- Give your notification a name – such as 'New caches' – and then choose a type of cache to watch by selecting from a drop-down menu – such as 'Traditional cache'.
- An additional list now appears with 12 options. If you want to receive only notifications of new caches, simply select 'Publish listing'.
- You need to select the co-ordinates that form the centre of the cache search area. This will default to your home co-ordinates, but you can reset it to a new location if you're searching for caches away from your home location. If you have not yet set your home co-ordinates, see Chapter 3.
- Set the distance from your home co-ordinates that you want to receive information about, for example 10km (the default is 20km, although there appears to be no limit to the distance you can set).
- Check 'Enable notifications'.
- Select 'Create notification'.

You will now receive an email every time a new cache meeting your criteria is published. If you want more than one type of cache you can set up multiple notifications.

Whitby Bay is the location of a number of caches linked to Bram Stoker, creator of *Dracula*

# 10 EVENTS, ACTIVITIES AND EVEN MORE ADVANCED STUFF

This final chapter covers a wide range of miscellaneous topics, all of which are relevant to the pursuit of geocaching in some way. While the following activities are all incidental to the core activity of geocaching, becoming involved in one or more of them will only serve to enhance the experience.

Geocaching is a worldwide activity – only about 160,000 of the 2.4 million worldwide caches are in the UK. Searching for caches in other countries is exactly the same as in the UK (but see Chapter 5, 'Search strategies', on using downloaded GPS co-ordinates overseas), although there is no guarantee that the cache page contents will be in English, so you may have to resort to Google Translate (www.translate.google.com) to figure out the clues. The weekly Groundspeak newsletter contains information about event caches worldwide, enabling you to meet with other geocachers while on holiday!

## GETTING INVOLVED, HAVING FUN AND JOINING A LOCAL ORGANISATION

Geocaching can be very much a solitary endeavour. Yet there is considerable pleasure in getting involved with other geocachers in your own area. If local events are organised they become 'Event caches', at which your attendance scores you a point in your overall tally of caches found. The easiest way to find out about events in your area is to set up an Instant Notification (see Chapter 9), selecting 'Event caches'. In this way you can be sure that as soon as an event's published you'll receive an email telling you about it.

Geocaching events are popular social occasions; some may involve a quick bout of geocaching followed by a convivial afternoon or evening in a local pub. Others may be timed to coincide with, for example, the twice-yearly equinoxes or some historical event of local significance, or they might take the form of a few hours' birdwatching at a local reserve, or the celebration of someone's birthday or other significant event. Each year there's a main 'MEGA Event' where the attendance exceeds 500; these are supported by a number of other events such as 'Piratemania'. The range of possibilities is limited only by imagination.

One way to enhance your geocaching experience is by joining a local group. These are not widespread across the

10

A group of geocachers set off across Morecambe Bay with Queen's Guide Cedric Robinson MBE as part of an event cache

UK, but currently are strongest in the north-west of England and the south-east; others certainly will evolve.

On website forums users can pose questions, raise issues or simply ask for advice about GPS devices, techniques, equipment and so on, or even about difficult caches. There are a number of other groups and forums from which you can glean information: these are listed on the GAGB Regional Forums page (www.gagb.co.uk/regional_links.php).

Groundspeak also has a range of forums, which have a worldwide audience. They can be accessed via 'Forums' in the left-hand column of the www.geocaching.com home page.

## MERCHANDISING
Groundspeak has an online 'shop' selling a wide range of geocaching products. It's accessible from the www.geocaching.com home page via 'Shop for gear'. (This book gives a list of UK online outlets in Appendix D.)

## YOSM CACHES (YE OLE SURVEY MONUMENTS)
[Thanks are due to Bernie Hughes (agentmancuso) for permission to include the following section, which was originally written by the author but based on an earlier text by Bernie, some of which remains.]

For many geocachers, the joy is the hunt and the find – Tupperware tracking – and that is often quite enough. But one of the pleasures of geocaching is that there are number of 'Add-ons': additional activities that – if plastic boxes aren't enough – significantly enhance the pursuit.

'Ye Ole Survey Monuments' (YOSMs, for short) are a perfect example. As those cachers who venture into the hills will know, there are quite a few caches close to trigpoints – those triangulation pillars erected by Ordnance Survey during the first half of the 20th century. But one cache has a special relationship with trigpoints: GC45CC (Ye Ole Survey Monuments). Owned by Canadian cacher outforthehunt, this is a virtual cache – a type of cache that still exists, but for which new caches are no longer accepted. This particular cache, however, is also a traveller, and moves around Britain, settling on a random trig pillar and staying there for a short time (usually two to three weeks) before moving on again.

So, you might ask, how did it come about that someone as far away as Canada should own such a significant British cache? Well, perhaps you've noticed that on www.geocaching.com it's also possible to log Benchmarks. Unfortunately, only US Benchmarks are listed, which leaves non-Americans out in the cold (unless you have the time, money and inclination to travel to America just to pick up an extra icon on your profile). Many Canadian cachers were disgruntled by this geocaching UDI, so outforthehunt set up a travelling virtual called Brass Cap Cache, which visits Canadian benchmarks (known as 'Brass Caps') and allows these to be counted in geocaching totals. The YOSM cache extends this idea to Britain, allowing cachers here to count trigpoint visits in our totals – though only once the trig has been listed by YOSM!

The YOSM virtual cache can be logged at any of the triangulation stations it has visited, not just the current one (which seems a bit odd). You may be logging your visit to a cache near you, but the current cache page is showing, for example, Bex Hill, or the Old Man of Coniston. This doesn't matter; although for its duration on the cache page you might be credited with having visited Bex Hill or the Old Man of Coniston, once that changes so will the record of your visit. The only thing to remember is not to add your YOSM cache visits to any mileage record you might be keeping, because that really will play havoc with the statistics.

More than 500 trigpoints have been visited by YOSM, and it even has its own website where a list of sites can be downloaded. You can get a nice badge for your profile here too, such as this one: www.yosm.org.uk/statpics/countrymatters.png.

There's also a league table of YOSM cachers, and over 1700 other cachers have so far taken part, more than 550 of whom have logged more than one visit.

10

**How to do it**

- GC45CC (YOSM) is logged in the usual way, with a 'Found it' log on www.geocaching.com, but repeat logs count towards your 'total finds' tally.
- YOSM can be, and usually is, logged retrospectively. The only stipulation is that the date of your visit should be subsequent to the initial publishing date of the cache in October 2003. If your trig visit was prior to October 2003, then you have to revisit.
- A complete list of YOSM trigs is downloadable as a GPX file from www.yosm.org.uk for use in Geocaching Swiss Army Knife (GSAK – see below) or equivalent.
- When logging on www.geocaching.com, include the YSM code, trig name and type (for example, 'YSM424 Trink Hill pillar'). This way your log will automatically be counted in the YOSM league table. If you then want to continue your log entry and say something about your visit, start on a new line to keep things tidy.

Only trigs that have been selected by outforthehunt count towards YOSM, but he has proved willing to accommodate requests for a specific trig to be added for special occasions and such.

## MUNZEES

A 'Munzee' is a QR-style barcode that's placed at a location. You go to the location by following the GPS co-ordinates for that Munzee, and 'capture' it by scanning the barcode using the Munzee app (essentially a QR-code reader).

The Munzee website (www.munzee.com) claims to 'take geocaching to the next level', but Munzees are in no way associated with Groundspeak. There are currently (2013) over 800,000 Munzees deployed, although many seem to be randomly placed rather than with aesthetic consideration.

To capture a Munzee you need an Android, iPhone or Windows smartphone that supports the Munzee app. As well as allowing you to capture Munzees, the app enables you to locate them and view a map on which they're dotted, much like the Geocaching apps. Munzees you've found show in red, while those you're yet to find show in green.

To deploy a Munzee, simply choose to create one on the website and a unique QR-code will be generated. Print this out – maybe laminate or cover it – and then place it somewhere appropriate. While at GZ, use the app to deploy the Munzee and it will be added to the website; you can edit the note and location right there and then, or you can do it later on the website. It's possible to buy pre-printed weatherproof Munzees from a number of online sources.

There are a few rules on where you can place Munzees, such as not on airport property, not within 500ft of a school or playground, and at a 'reasonable distance' from other Munzees.

After capturing a Munzee you're awarded points; when anyone captures a Munzee that you've deployed you also get points, and your 'level' increases, pushing you higher up the leader board in the rankings.

Munzees have the potential to replace the no-longer-accepted (but much-loved) 'virtual' caches of www. geocaching.com, but in a parallel universe.

## BENCHMARKING

Benchmarks are vertical control stations used by Ordnance Survey for measuring elevation, and their position is known by Ordnance Survey to a high degree of accuracy. The search for benchmarks is an add-on activity allied to geo-caching. The development of searches for benchmarks originated in the US, and much of the information on the www. geocaching.com website is US-related. But it's an additional and moderate interest that can be pursued by geocachers in the UK.

Benchmarks in the UK are most noticeable in two forms: a cut benchmark engraved into stone, and the same shape embossed into a small bracket (known as a flush bracket) affixed to the base of Ordnance Survey trig pillars, which carry a unique identifying number (S1543, for example, is the trig-pillar bracket on the summit of Skiddaw in the Lake District).

Flush brackets were first used during the Second Geodetic Levelling of England and Wales (2GL) between 1912 and 1921. The 2GL brackets were numbered 1 to 3000, and the vast majority of these brackets were placed on walls and buildings, with only a small number (only 46, in the range 2943 to 2999) being affixed to triangulation pillars. There's a greater number of a different type of bracket, known as the S-bracket because they're prefixed with the letter 'S'. These range from S01 to S9999, and were introduced in 1920. This series also includes a number of brackets numbered 10,000 and higher, but without the 'S' prefix. A G-series of flush brackets first appeared in 1936, at the commencement of the Second Geodetic Levelling of Scotland, and these are found exclusively on walls. Finally, a small series of just 16 brackets (the L-series – L1 to L16) was affixed during the Re-levelling of Greater London from 1931 to 1934.

Benchmarks can be found at various locations all over the UK, and you can discover UK benchmarks via the Ordnance Survey Bench Mark Database at www.bench-marks.org.uk.

**S-series flush bracket**

**Bolt benchmark**

**Cut benchmark**

EVENTS, ACTIVITIES AND EVEN MORE ADVANCED STUFF

10

You can search locally by using your postcode; go to the website and enter your postcode into the 'Search' box, and a list of benchmarks near you will appear. Or you can select 'Search' from the header menu of the database and define the type of benchmarks you're looking for. Your benchmark finds can be logged on www.waymarking.com.

## WAYMARKING

Waymarking is similar to geocaching, but with waymarking there are no physical cache containers. The pursuit centres on points of interest, such as buildings, vehicles, monuments, signs, structures (such as canal bridges), mountain summits, places of recreation or entertainment, and even weird story locations. Given this width of potential, it's not surprising that there are thousands of waymarks across the UK.

Historically, what are today known as 'waymarks' used to be loggable on www.geocaching.com in the category 'Locationless reverse' (such as GCCF43: World Heritage). But this category is no longer used. Locationless caches are the opposite of a traditional cache. Instead of finding a hidden container, you're given a task to locate a specific object and log its co-ordinates. In about 2005, Groundspeak decided to archive all locationless caches, but as a result all these caches became categories on a website dedicated to waymarking – www.waymarking.com – and the pursuit of waymarking started from there. You can use this website to discover the waymarks near you.

## SUMMIT CACHING

These caches were originally created by and for radio amateurs taking part in the 'Summits of the Air' (SOTA) programme. Numerous hill summits in Britain were cata-logued, and radio hams 'activated' them by transmitting from the summits. But because of the difficulty in carrying radio equipment to the top of a hill, it was decided to create conventional caches on some (but not all) summits. Radio hams could now obtain credit for finding them as official geocaches, rather than needing to transmit from the summit. And because they're physical caches, they can be searched for by geocachers too.

The summit caching website – www.summitcaching. org.uk – includes summit tables showing the number of finders of each 'cache', along with annual and overall league tables, should you wish to join in this pursuit. As the caches are hidden on mountain tops, geocachers who are also hill walkers will find this an interesting addition to the basic pursuit of geocaching. Some are easy to find and some are difficult, especially under winter conditions and bad weather. This activity is independent of and not an official part of the SOTA programme.

Summits where it has not been possible to place a geocache – perhaps because there's already a geocache in close proximity – have been registered as waymarks (see above).

## TRIGPOINTING

Trigpoints – the familiar name for triangulation pillars – are the Ordnance Survey obelisks dotted around the countryside. These concrete pillars, about 4ft tall, were used by the Ordnance Survey to survey the landscape of the country in order to create detailed maps. They're usually, but not exclusively, located on the highest point of ground in an area so that there's a direct line of sight from one to the next. By sitting a theodolite (an accurate compass built into a telescope) on the top of the pillar, exact bearings to nearby trigpoints could be taken. No longer required for active service, many trigpoints have been adopted by individuals who have taken over responsibility for their upkeep. Each of these 'trigs' originally had what is known as a flush bracket – a metal plate, attached to the pillar, carrying a unique reference number and a benchmark.

Cadair Idris in Snowdonia has a typical summit cache

10

**Trigpointing on the Isle of Mull**

The practice of 'bagging' trigpoints is another add-on feature of geocaching. The search for many geocaches will lead you past trigpoints, so it becomes a logical extension of geocaching to make a note of the numbers on trig pillars, and then to log them on www.trigpointinguk.com – a dedicated website. However, bear in mind that many trigpoints are on private land to which there is no access other than by courtesy of the landowner.

## CACHE STATISTICS

The geocaching website hosts all the information about caches that you've found or placed. As the number of caches you discover increases, keeping track of those that you were the first to find (FTF), or those of varying levels of difficulty and terrain, becomes complicated. However, there are a few ways in which all this data can be harnessed and collated in a meaningful way.

Begin by going to 'Pocket Queries' under 'Your Profile'. Select 'Add to Queue' under 'My Finds' at the foot of the page. Once you've added a PQ to the queue, wait for the result to arrive by email as a zip file. (But before opening the zip file, save it to your computer.) Downloaded zip files should automatically be directed to the 'Unzipped' folder

On your computer create a folder called 'Geocaching', and get into the habit of placing anything relating to geocaching in there.

in your 'Downloads' folder, but in addition you should save a copy of the unopened zip file to your geocaching folder.

Now you need to download software (free) that will manage the data from the PQ. CacheStats is one format, and this is downloadable from www.logicweave.com.

Having downloaded the data management software, you now need to give it the PQ data to manipulate:

- Unzip the zip file. This creates a GPX file. Your computer will automatically place this in the 'Unzipped' folder, but you may want to redirect it to your geocaching folder, and you will be given the opportunity to do this during the unzipping process.
- Now run the CacheStats software, during the course of which you'll be asked to 'Open a GPX file'. Use this to locate and open the file, and the software will then produce tables of statistics that show your progress, including yearly data, a calendar of your geocaching activity, significant milestones, locations, size/type of caches found, difficult and terrain and a D/T grid (see below).

## D/T GRID

Geocaching, as you've probably realised by now, is about challenges. One particular form of challenge is to find caches that meet every combination of difficulty and terrain. This is shown on a D/T grid, sometimes also called a '9x9 grid' or a D/T square.

The object of the D/T grid is, of course, to complete it – something that most geocachers do in part. But finding the most difficult caches is a challenge in itself; there are even a few caches (such as GC1JTG4: NineSquared) that you can find only when you've completed the D/T grid. It's all part of the fun.

| | | | | Terrain | | | | | | |
|---|---|---|---|---|---|---|---|---|---|---|
| | | 1 | 1.5 | 2 | 2.5 | 3 | 3.5 | 4 | 4.5 | 5 | |
| **Difficulty** | 1 | 176 | 145 | 59 | 29 | 25 | 10 | 7 | 2 | 1 | 454 |
| | 1.5 | 110 | 860 | 241 | 132 | 58 | 31 | 22 | 6 | 3 | **1463** |
| | 2 | 58 | 326 | 457 | 160 | 138 | 67 | 34 | 10 | 4 | 1254 |
| | 2.5 | 19 | 110 | 83 | 113 | 37 | 16 | 15 | 8 | 3 | 404 |
| | 3 | 9 | 68 | 44 | 29 | 31 | 22 | 21 | 8 | 0 | 232 |
| | 3.5 | 5 | 17 | 16 | 4 | 4 | 2 | 8 | 2 | 0 | 58 |
| | 4 | 3 | 18 | 10 | 3 | 4 | 5 | 7 | 2 | 1 | 53 |
| | 4.5 | 4 | 2 | 0 | 0 | 2 | 3 | 2 | 1 | 1 | 15 |
| | 5 | 4 | 2 | 1 | 4 | 3 | 1 | 0 | 2 | 6 | 23 |
| | | 388 | **1548** | 911 | 474 | 302 | 157 | 116 | 41 | 19 | **3956** |

D/T grid

10

## EARTHCACHE MASTER PROGRAMME

The EarthCache element of geocaching is designed to help people understand the Earth in a geological context. Seeking out EarthCaches is an opportunity for all the family to learn something about the landscape and its creation. The listing of EarthCache sites is done by the Geological Society of America.

**EARTHCACHE MASTER**
BRONZE LEVEL

As part of the process of acquiring EarthCaches, you have the chance to become part of the EarthCache Master's programme. There are four EarthCache Master levels: bronze, silver, gold and platinum.

- **Bronze EarthCache Master** – you must visit and log three or more EarthCaches in two or more countries (Scotland, England, Wales and Northern Ireland count as separate countries for this purpose).
- **Silver EarthCache Master** – visit and log six or more EarthCaches in three or more countries, and develop one or more EarthCaches of your own.
- **Gold EarthCache Master** – visit and log 12 or more EarthCaches in four or more countries, and develop two or more EarthCaches.
- **Platinum EarthCache Master** – visit and log 20 or more EarthCaches in five or more countries, and develop three or more EarthCaches.

Information about EarthCaches can be found at www. earthcache.org, which is run by the organisation to which you submit your claims to the different levels of membership.

## GEOCACHING CO-ORDINATES CHECKER

If you place a cache that requires someone to solve a puzzle before arriving at the correct co-ordinates, you can use www.geochecker.com to allow people to check that they've correctly solved the puzzle. As a cache owner, you enter the cache name and cache code along with the correct co-ordinates. Then you create a code, which links to your cache page and allows puzzle solvers to check their work.

This website also lists the 25 most popular puzzles, along with the 25 hardest puzzles (not all of them in the UK).

## ALTERNATIVE GEOCACHING SYSTEMS

The website www.geocaching.com is not the only geocaching database; there are four other systems, the evolution of which is not always clear or satisfactorily explained. All, in terms of volume of caches, are substantially inferior to www. geocaching.com, but provide geocachers with a choice.

Although as yet of limited extent (fewer than 1000 caches in the UK), www.opencaching.org.uk is a UK-specific database that operates on similar principles to www.geocaching.com, but is confined to caches located in the UK. There are similar Opencaching sites in Finland, Germany, Poland and the Czech Republic (www.opencaching.eu), as well as in Australia, Hungary, Estonia, Romania, Turkey and Russia.

Not to be confused with Opencaching.org.uk, **Opencaching** (www.opencaching.com) is another geocaching database, in this case managed by Garmin. This system operates in much the same way as the others, but has no subscription, and caches are not reviewed by a team of reviewers but by the membership itself. While not restricted to the UK, most of the UK caches are in England, with only a small number extending into Northern Ireland, Scotland and Wales.

The distinction between Garmin's OpenCaching and OpenCaching.org.uk is that the former functions across many different localised sites, specifically run to be open and accessible to everyone. Garmin's OpenCaching is proprietary (like www.geocaching.com), although currently (2013) it has no fees for membership.

**TerraCaching** (www.terracaching.com) is yet another worldwide system, with the stated aims of creating and supporting a semi-open community of serious and responsible cachers; providing tools that actively encourage and reward members for placing high quality, enjoyable caches; providing a unique list of caches, not listed elsewhere, that meet high standards of quality; and providing an atmosphere of friendly competition among members.

## GEOCACHING RESOURCES
There are a number of online resources to help geocachers old and new.

### Geocaching Association of Great Britain
The Geocaching Association of Great Britain (GAGB) was set up by a group of experienced geocachers in response to a perceived need for an association to represent geocaching in the UK at a national level; to enhance geocaching in the UK; and to facilitate its progress.

It does this by:
- liaising with local and national landowning bodies, and agreeing guidelines so that caching on their land is approved and encouraged
- helping all members to enjoy the activity without falling foul of the civil and criminal laws of the land
- establishing good caching practices by accepting advice from land, environmental, archaeological and historical bodies

EVENTS, ACTIVITIES AND EVEN MORE ADVANCED STUFF

**10**

- acting as an intermediary and as the first point of call for all interested parties in the UK
- ensuring that the positive educational, environmental and recreational aspects of geocaching are properly represented
- helping new members of the geocaching community as necessary.

The Association:

- negotiates with major owners of publicly accessible land in Great Britain for a positive approach to geocaching
- encourages appropriate publicity to promote geocaching
- maintains a page of links to websites containing information on environmental, legal and other topics of interest to geocachers
- has developed a definitive set of geocaching guidelines specific to Great Britain
- has developed a reference system to summarise laws and other issues that impact on geocaching in Great Britain
- publishes a bi-monthly magazine – *Seeker* – which provides information about geocaching generally, equipment, activities, and geocaching destinations.

Over the years, GAGB has negotiated agreements with major landowners for permission to carry out geocaching on their land. A list of all landowners who allow geocaching, and those who do not, appears on its website (www.gagb.org.uk). Some, but not all, of these landowners require you to get permission using a specific application form; these forms can be downloaded from the website.

### Follow the Arrow

This website (www.follow-the-arrow.co.uk), designed by an existing geocacher, provides help and information about using geocaching technology, and about geocaching generally. The site includes information about paperless caching, how GPSrs work, and a comparison/buying guide.

### UK Geocaching Wiki

This Wiki (http://wiki.groundspeak.com) provides a number of links to other useful sites; a map of regional boundaries (to be used when creating a new cache); mapping resources, including a number of interactive maps; details on how to go about getting permission to place a cache; and links to the various national and regional forums.

## MAGIC Map

Multi Agency Geographic Information for the Countryside, primarily for England, is a government-sponsored map that allows you to view detailed maps of the UK and overlay on them various coloured layers of land areas where permission to place caches is required. It's a useful tool for checking whether the place you're intending to put a cache is in any way protected, for example local nature reserves, National Nature Reserves, Sites of Special Scientific Interest (SSSIs), Scheduled Ancient Monuments, National Trust land, Forestry Commission estates, Woodland Trust properties and RSPB reserves.

The map is most usefully opened through www.benchmarks.org.uk/magicmapit.php, since this reveals all categories of protected area; if you access MAGIC Map manually, you'll have to select each layer of designation to be sure your intended location is not protected.

## PROJECT-GC

This is an online web service that is meant to help geocachers in fun and useful ways by providing both geocaching statistics (including your own) and helpful tools (www.project-gc.com).

## Geocaching Swiss Army Knife

The Geocaching Swiss Army Knife (GSAK) is an all-in-one geocaching and waypoint management tool. Major features include multiple databases; sending/receiving waypoints to GPS; Google Maps; conversion to many mapping formats; iPhone/BlackBerry output; HTML output; extensive searching; macro support; backup and restore; distance/direction from other waypoints (including caches, locations, postcodes) and much more. GSAK runs only on Windows operating systems (98, ME, NT, 2000, XP, Vista and Windows 7).

GSAK is a more sophisticated version of cache statistic programs, and has much greater functionality. Its various complexities, however, are likely to prove of benefit only to geocachers who've established a good level of understanding of the way geocaching works. Once achieved, the benefits of GSAK can be more readily understood. It's beyond the scope of this book to explain the whole range of GSAK possibilities, but the software is available from www.gsak.net. There is a free version, although the one-off cost of registering for a paid version is nominal, and is not restricted to one computer.

10

# Appendix A
# UNDERSTANDING GEO-SPEAK

As with many activities, a dedicated language has evolved for geocaching, much of it abbreviated to initial letters. The language is evolving all the time. Here is a basic glossary of terms:

**archived**: describes a cache that no longer exists (for a variety of reasons), but which still appears in the database for historical purposes. A cache might be archived because it has been lost, is no longer maintained by the owner, or does not abide by the guidelines determining where and how caches may be placed.

**BYOP**: 'bring your own pen' is a way of letting cachers know that the container is too small to hold a pen provided by the cache owner… so, bring your own.

**cache and dash**: (*aka* drive-by) is a cache that's placed close to a convenient parking spot, from which you can quickly dash to the cache location.

**CITO**: 'Cache In, Trash Out'

**CO**: cache owner

**D/T**: stands for the difficulty and terrain rating of a cache

**day grid**: the display within your 'Statistics' that shows the days on which you've been geocaching. After a while, it becomes a challenge to complete a day grid fully; the key is to ensure that in a leap year you find a cache on 29 February!

**DNF**: 'Did not find'. Using DNF when you log your search on www.geocaching.com records the fact that you were unable to find the cache. It also alerts the owner to the possibility that the cache may be missing.

**drive-by**: see 'cache and dash'

**event cache**: a formal or informal get-together of geocachers, which may range from a pie and a pint in a pub to an organised collective search for caches or a multi-day event.

**FTF**: 'First to find'. A simple message entered in the log by the first person to find a cache. Sometimes 2TF ('Second to find') is also used, but after that it becomes meaningless.

**GC code**: the cache code, allocated by the system

**GPS**: Global Positioning System (system of satellites)

**GPSr**: slang for a GPS device

**GSAK**: Geocaching Swiss Army Knife – a geocaching management tool

**GZ**: 'Ground Zero' – the spot where the cache co-ordinates and those on your GPS are a match. Note, however, that the cache may not always be at GZ because the co-ordinates may be out by a small amount.

**hitchhiker**: an object that moves from cache to cache, marked with some instructions, telling the finder what to do with it; also known as a 'traveller'

**muggle**: a term borrowed from the *Harry Potter* books to refer to people who are not geocachers

**PAF**: 'Phone a friend'. PAF signifies that the cache was difficult to find, and that the finder succeeded only by telephoning another geocacher who had already found the cache. This is done not so much to receive the exact whereabouts of the cache, but to get additional information or help. Also TAF: 'Text a friend'.

**paperless caching**: as its name suggests, paperless caching is caching without having to print out the cache page description. Instead, using a GPX file, you download all the cache page details directly to a GPSr or smartphone.

**ROT13**: the basic encryption system used by www.geocaching.com, where each of the letters is rotated 13 characters up or down in the alphabet

**SL**: 'Signed log'. Entered on the website to signify that the finder signed the log contained in the cache

**spoiler**: information or a photograph that might give away the exact location of a cache

**SWAG**: acronym standing for 'Stuff We All Get'. Includes trade items left in caches

**TFTC**: 'Thanks for the cache' – a courtesy note left when logging a find on the website

**TNLN**: 'Took nothing, left nothing' – note left on the website that signifies that the finder took nothing from the cache and placed nothing in it. Many finders enter 'TFTC TNLN SL' on the website.

**waypoint**: a location, expressed in the same format as cache co-ordinates, that relates not to the cache itself but to a useful feature – such as a convenient car park or a bridge – that might be useful in reaching the cache location.

# Appendix B
# THE NATIONAL COUNTRY CODES

England and Wales, and Scotland, have their own official codes outlining the responsibilities of anyone enjoying the countryside, whether it be in national parks, access land or common land, and these codes express the same general principles. The following points are a summary of the Countryside Code for England and Wales:

- **Be safe – plan ahead and follow any signs**
  Even when going out locally, it's best to get the latest information about where and when you can go; for example, your rights to go onto some areas of open land may be restricted while work is carried out, for safety reasons or during breeding seasons. Follow advice and local signs, and be prepared for the unexpected.
- **Protect plants and animals, and take your litter home**
  We have a responsibility to protect our countryside, now and for future generations, so make sure you don't harm animals, birds, plants or trees.
- **Keep dogs under close control**
  The countryside is a great place to exercise dogs, but it's every owner's duty to make sure their dog is not a danger or nuisance to farm animals, wildlife or other people.
- **Leave gates and property as you find them**
  Please respect the working life of the countryside; our actions can affect people's livelihoods, our heritage, and the safety and welfare of animals and ourselves.
- **Consider other people**
  Showing consideration and respect for other people makes the countryside a pleasant environment for everyone – at home, at work and at leisure.

The full version of the Countryside Code for England and Wales is available online at www.naturalengland. org.uk/ourwork/enjoying/countrysidecode, while the Scottish Outdoor Access Code is available at www. outdooraccess-scotland.com. There is no official code for Northern Ireland, but the outdoor ethics programme Leave No Trace promotes a similar ethos in its 'seven principles', available at www.leavenotraceireland.org.

# Appendix C
# ACCESS TO THE COUNTRYSIDE: WALKERS AND THE LAW

Geocaching in the UK can take place almost anywhere, from town centres to remote mountain tops – although there tend to be restrictions (or at least careful control) over the placement of geocaches in environmentally sensitive areas and other places where there's an actual or perceived danger. The guidelines for placing caches are contained elsewhere, but the opportunity is taken here to give a brief summary of the law of access – that is, the freedom to roam – particularly as it applies to the open countryside, although this is not a definitive statement of the law.

The mere fact that a cache exists does not mean that you have access to it other than within the law; in other words, you are not at liberty to commit a trespass or cause damage in pursuit of a cache – you have to get there lawfully.

## ENGLAND AND WALES

The law relating to access in England and Wales is enshrined in the Countryside and Rights of Way Act, 2000, usually shortened to the 'CRoW Act, 2000'.

Until the passing of the CRoW Act, walkers could legally access the countryside only along rights of way: public footpaths, bridleways, and Byways Open to All Traffic (BOATs). The CRoW Act amended existing legislation to provide for access on foot to certain categories of land – notably mountain, moor, heath, down and common land. In effect, this means that walkers now have access to large areas of open land. There's no restriction on continuing to use existing rights of way; the difference is that you may now leave the right of way and wander freely – but only within those areas designated as Access Land. These are shown on Ordnance Survey maps by a yellow tint within a pale orange border.

This freedom to roam gives geocachers the opportunity to place caches in remote locations, which they frequently do (often far from convenient paths). In this respect geocachers differ from recreational walkers, not least because existing pathways follow the driest and surest routes across land; the fact that you can wander anywhere on Access Land is not always the benefit it may seem.

## SCOTLAND

The situation in Scotland is slightly different. Here, walkers have always taken access, by custom, tradition or right, over most land. The law in Scotland is now embodied in the Land Reform (Scotland) Act, 2003, which came into effect in February 2005.

The Land Reform (Scotland) Act, 2003 tells you where rights of access apply in Scotland, while the Scottish Outdoor Access Code sets out your responsibilities when exercising these rights. These responsibilities can be summarised as follows:

- take responsibility for your own actions;
- respect the interests of other people, and
- care for the environment.

Access rights can be exercised over most land and inland water in Scotland by all non-motorised users, including walkers, cyclists, horse riders and canoeists – providing they do so responsibly. Walkers and others must behave in ways that are compatible with land management needs, and land managers also have reciprocal responsibilities to manage their land to facilitate access, taken either by right, custom or tradition. Local authorities and national park authorities have a duty and the powers to uphold access rights.

People may be requested not to take access for certain periods of time; for example, when tree-felling is taking place, during the stalking season, or for nature conservation reasons. It is responsible to comply with reasonable requests. Access rights also extend to lightweight, informal camping.

Farmyards are not included in the right of access, but you may still take access through farmyards by rights-of-way, custom or tradition. Farmers are encouraged to sign alternative routes if they do not want people passing through their farmyard. If you are going through a farmyard, proceed with care and respect the privacy of those living on the farm.

## NORTHERN IRELAND

Northern Ireland has very few public rights of way and therefore in many areas walkers enjoy the countryside only by the goodwill and tolerance of landowners.

Much of Northern Ireland's public land, such as Water Service and Forest Service land, is also accessible, as is land owned and managed by organisations such as the National Trust and the Woodland Trust.

# Appendix D
# ONLINE SUPPLIERS IN THE UK

**Above & Beyond**
Tel: 0845 257 2675
Email: sales@aboveandbeyond.co.uk
www.aboveandbeyond.co.uk

**Base of Tree**
www.baseoftree.com

**GeocacheKit**
Email: admin@geocachekit.co.uk
www.geocachekit.co.uk

**Geotastic**
Tel: 0844 887 0652
www.geotastic.com

**Geotees**
www.geotees.co.uk and www.geotees.eu

**NE Geocaching Supplies**
Tel: 07756 702732
www.negeocachingsupplies.co.uk

**Pulse 72 Geocaching**
Tel: 07900 155888
www.pulse72geocaching.co.uk

**UKGeocachers**
Tel: 07780 118185
Email: admin@ukgeocachers.co.uk
www.ukgeocachers.co.uk

**Skyblue Leisure**
Tel: 01637 872951
www.skyblueleisure.co.uk

**The Geocaching Shop**
www.thegeocachingshop.com

# INDEX

INDEX

# LISTING OF CICERONE GUIDES

Cycling in the French Alps
Cycling the Canal du Midi
Cycling the River Loire
The Danube Cycleway
The Grand Traverse of the Massif Central
The Moselle Cycle Route
The Rhine Cycle Route
The Way of St James

**AFRICA**

Climbing in the Moroccan Anti-Atlas
Kilimanjaro
Mountaineering in the Moroccan High Atlas
The High Atlas
Trekking in the Atlas Mountains
Walking in the Drakensberg

**ALPS – CROSS-BORDER ROUTES**

100 Hut Walks in the Alps
Across the Eastern Alps: E5
Alpine Points of View
Alpine Ski Mountaineering
1 Western Alps
2 Central and Eastern Alps
Chamonix to Zermatt
Snowshoeing
Tour of Mont Blanc
Tour of Monte Rosa
Tour of the Matterhorn
Trekking in the Alps
Trekking in the Silvretta and Rätikon Alps
Walking in the Alps
Walks and Treks in the Maritime Alps

**PYRENEES AND FRANCE/SPAIN CROSS-BORDER ROUTES**

Rock Climbs in the Pyrenees
The GR10 Trail
The GR11 Trail – La Senda
The Mountains of Andorra
The Pyrenean Haute Route
The Pyrenees
The Way of St James
Walks and Climbs in the Pyrenees

**AUSTRIA**

The Adlerweg
Trekking in Austria's Hohe Tauern
Trekking in the Stubai Alps
Trekking in the Zillertal Alps
Walking in Austria

**EASTERN EUROPE**

The High Tatras
The Mountains of Romania
Walking in Bulgaria's National Parks
Walking in Hungary

**FRANCE**

Chamonix Mountain Adventures
Ecrins National Park
GR20: Corsica
Mont Blanc Walks
Mountain Adventures in the Maurienne
The Cathar Way
The GR20 Corsica
The GR5 Trail
The Robert Louis Stevenson Trail
Tour of the Oisans: The GR54
Tour of the Queyras
Tour of the Vanoise
Trekking in the Vosges and Jura
Vanoise Ski Touring
Via Ferratas of the French Alps
Walking in Corsica
Walking in Provence – East
Walking in Provence – West
Walking in the Auvergne
Walking in the Cathar Region
Walking in the Cevennes
Walking in the Dordogne
Walking in the Haute Savoie
Walking in the Languedoc
Walking in the Tarentaise and Beaufortain Alps

**GERMANY**

Germany's Romantic Road
Hiking and Biking in the Black Forest
Walking in the Bavarian Alps
Walking the River Rhine Trail

**HIMALAYA**

Annapurna
Bhutan
Everest
Garhwal and Kumaon
Langtang with Gosainkund and Helambu
Manaslu
The Mount Kailash Trek
Trekking in Ladakh
Trekking in the Himalaya

**ICELAND & GREENLAND**

Trekking in Greenland
Walking and Trekking in Iceland

**IRELAND**

Irish Coastal Walks
The Irish Coast to Coast Walk
The Mountains of Ireland

**ITALY**

Gran Paradiso
Sibillini National Park
Stelvio National Park
Shorter Walks in the Dolomites
Through the Italian Alps
Trekking in the Apennines
Trekking in the Dolomites
Via Ferratas of the Italian Dolomites: Vols 1 & 2
Walking in Abruzzo
Walking in Sardinia
Walking in Sicily
Walking in the Central Italian Alps
Walking in the Dolomites
Walking in Tuscany
Walking in Umbria
Walking on the Amalfi Coast
Walking the Italian Lakes

**MEDITERRANEAN**

Jordan – Walks, Treks, Caves, Climbs and Canyons
The Ala Dag
The High Mountains of Crete
The Mountains of Greece
Treks and Climbs in Wadi Rum
Walking in Malta
Western Crete

**NORTH AMERICA**

British Columbia
The Grand Canyon
The John Muir Trail
The Pacific Crest Trail

**SOUTH AMERICA**

Aconcagua and the Southern Andes
Hiking and Biking Peru's Inca Trails
Torres del Paine

**SCANDINAVIA**

Walking in Norway

**SLOVENIA, CROATIA AND MONTENEGRO**

The Islands of Croatia
The Julian Alps of Slovenia
The Mountains of Montenegro
Trekking in Slovenia
Walking in Slovenia: The Karavanke

**SPAIN AND PORTUGAL**

Costa Blanca: West
Mountain Walking in Southern Catalunya
The Mountains of Central Spain
The Northern Caminos
Trekking through Mallorca
Walking in Madeira
Walking in Mallorca
Walking in Menorca
Walking in the Algarve
Walking in the Cordillera Cantabrica
Walking in the Sierra Nevada
Walking on Gran Canaria
Walking on La Gomera and El Hierro
Walking on La Palma
Walking on Tenerife
Walking the GR7 in Andalucia
Walks and Climbs in the Picos de Europa

**SWITZERLAND**

Alpine Pass Route
Central Switzerland
The Bernese Alps
The Swiss Alps
Tour of the Jungfrau Region
Walking in the Valais
Walking in Ticino
Walks in the Engadine

**TECHNIQUES**

Geocaching in the UK
Indoor Climbing
Lightweight Camping
Map and Compass
Mountain Weather
Moveable Feasts
Outdoor Photography
Polar Exploration
Rock Climbing
Sport Climbing
The Book of the Bivvy
The Hillwalker's Guide to Mountaineering
The Hillwalker's Manual

**MINI GUIDES**

Alpine Flowers
Avalanche!
Navigating with a GPS
Navigation
Pocket First Aid and Wilderness Medicine
Snow

**MOUNTAIN LITERATURE**

8000m
A Walk in the Clouds
Unjustifiable Risk?

For full information on all our guides, books and eBooks, visit our website: www.cicerone.co.uk.

# Walking – Trekking – Mountaineering – Climbing – Cycling

**Over 40 years, Cicerone have built up an outstanding collection of 300 guides, inspiring all sorts of amazing adventures.**

Every guide comes from extensive exploration and research by our expert authors, all with a passion for their subjects. They are frequently praised, endorsed and used by clubs, instructors and outdoor organisations.

All our titles can now be bought as **e-books** and many as iPad and Kindle files and we will continue to make all our guides available for these and many other devices.

Our website shows any **new information** we've received since a book was published. Please do let us know if you find anything has changed, so that we can pass on the latest details. On our **website** you'll also find some great ideas and lots of information, including sample chapters, contents lists, reviews, articles and a photo gallery.

It's easy to keep in touch with what's going on at Cicerone, by getting our monthly **free e-newsletter**, which is full of offers, competitions, up-to-date information and topical articles. You can subscribe on our home page and also follow us on **Facebook** and **Twitter**, as well as our **blog**.

**Cicerone – the very best guides for exploring the world.**

## CICERONE

2 Police Square  Milnthorpe  Cumbria  LA7 7PY
Tel: 015395 62069  info@cicerone.co.uk
**www.cicerone.co.uk**